THE DEITIES ARE MANY

SUNY series in Religious Studies
Harold Coward, editor

THE DEITIES ARE MANY

A Polytheistic Theology

Jordan Paper

STATE UNIVERSITY OF NEW YORK PRESS

Published by
State University of New York Press, Albany

© 2005 State University of New York

All rights reserved

Printed in the United States of America

No part of this book may be used or reproduced in any manner
whatsoever without written permission. No part of this book may be
stored in a retrieval system or transmitted in any form or by any
means including electronic, electrostatic, magnetic tape, mechanical,
photocopying, recording, or otherwise without the prior permission
in writing of the publisher.

For information, address State University of New York Press,
90 State Street, Suite 700, Albany, NY 12207

Production by Marilyn P. Semerad
Marketing by Susan M. Petrie

Library of Congress Cataloging-in-Publication Data

Paper, Jordan D.
    The deities are many : a polytheistic theology / Jordan Paper.
        p. cm.
    Includes index.
    ISBN 0–7914–6387–7 (hardcover)—ISBN 0–7914–6388–5 (pbk.)
    1. Polytheism.   2. Religions.   I. Title.
BL355.P36 2005
211′.32—dc22

                                                                2004007344

10 9 8 7 6 5 4 3 2 1

*For the African Bazilian,
Anishnabeg, Chinese, Japanese, and
Pikuni women and men who shared
their spiritual lives with me.*

CONTENTS

———❖———

One of the most wonderful things is the orixá [deities] ... *And
we feel confused and grateful at the same time, with this process
of having an* orixá ... *And I feel very much this force, this
major force, a force I can't explain. It exists between Heaven
and Earth ... There are mysteries that cannot be explained, and
one of them is the* orixá.

—Zeze, a young African Brazilian woman, in
the film *Candomblé: A Religion in Brazil with
African Roots* (1989), translated from the Portuguese

PREFACE

❖

For the last three decades of my scholarly career, along with other religionists, I have been insisting on a separation of religious studies, as a relatively objective study of an essential aspect of culture, from theology, as a subjective study of one's own belief structure. Most of my publications have involved the comparative study of religion with a focus on countering Eurocentric and androcentric biases in such studies. My approach has been that of participant-observation with the purpose of ascertaining the hermeneutics of the cultures studied. Yet my major publications in these regards—*Offering Smoke: The Sacred Pipe and Native American Religion* (University of Idaho Press, 1988), *The Spirits Are Drunk: Comparative Approaches to Chinese Religion* (State University of New York Press, 1995), and *Through the Earth Darkly: Female Spirituality in Comparative Perspective* (Continuum, 1997)—due to the nature of my participation was scientific in orientation and yet skirted advocacy because of the depth of my participation. And while I am still engaged in the scientific study of religion, my comparative studies have led me into comparative theology. But theology, by its very nature, is confessional. Hence, I have reached the point where my studies have compelled me to cross the line from religious studies to theology.

Decades of deep involvement in disparate religious traditions have provided me with a personal religious understanding that is, in itself, comparative. For this reason, some of my colleagues have encouraged me to write this treatise as a rather unusual contribution to the literature on religion, because I may be one of a very few scholars who can write a general rather than culturally specific confessional polytheistic theology. But I realize that other of my colleagues will shake their heads in disapproval, even more certain that participant-observation is a

dangerous and dubious methodology. In response, I would sug-
gest that the countering of Eurocentrism in the study of religion
means taking non-Western ideologies seriously. This work is
intended to demonstrate that the ideological bases of non-Western religions, all polytheistic when the effects of Western domination are removed, should be accepted by those studying
religion to be as genuine as the monotheistic basis of the Western religions.

The initial draft of this book was written nonstop in a single
month during the summer of 1999 at my cabin on Wasauksing
(Parry Island Reserve) in Georgian Bay (central Ontario), my last
summer there after many years before moving to the West
Coast. The revisions were written at my home by Willow Beach
in Oak Bay (Victoria) on the southern tip of Vancouver Island.
Hence, the reflections on Native American traditional understandings is germane to the Algonkian-speaking traditions of
the Great Lakes region and the Plains but not necessarily to the
traditions of the Northwest Coast.

ACKNOWLEDGMENTS

❖

So many people have been crucial to the understandings expressed here that it would be impractical, if not impossible, to list them all; many have been cited in the acknowledgments expressed in the three books of mine listed in the Preface. I would like to particularly thank, however, two colleagues whose encouragement immediately led to the writing of this book: Rita Gross and John Berthrong, the latter who, as well, pointed out some essential improvements to the text. Equally important has been the continuing stimulation and encouragement of my colleagues at York University, Johanna Stuckey, who carefully edited the initial manuscript, and Stephen Ford, who corrected my wording with regard to Christian theology. I would also like to acknowledge the enormous patience and tolerance, given my many years of involvement in a variety of rituals that often took me away from home, of my wife, Chuang Li, without whose support in so many ways this work would not have come into being.

Similarly, much of what I have written reflects, in varying ways, the work of many scholars before me, yet this work is being presented without references. This has been done for two reasons. First, to have acknowledged the indirect contribution of hundreds, if not thousands of sources, would have led to more pages of notes than of text. Second, I wrote this work without consulting other works; it was an outpouring within a short period of time of nearly a half century's' reflection on this work's theme. To go back and find all the potential references would have taken years of retroactive research. Most of the relevant works, however, again will be found cited in the three books listed in the Preface, and all would have been mentioned in one or more of my hundred or so publications.

Given that I have written a number of articles and sections of books on comparative theology, undoubtedly some sentences or even paragraphs to be found in this work will reflect earlier writings. This is inevitable given that my thinking on these issues has continued to develop in the same direction. But I cannot give credit to these potential, limited, partial repetitions, as they are from memory rather than explicitly copied.

The initial draft of this book was written while on sabbatical from York University to carry out research on the mystic experience: *The Mystic Experience: A Descriptive and Comparative Analysis* (State University of New York Press 2004). I am most appreciative of the support of the then dean of the Faculty of Arts, George Fallis, and the chair of the Division of Humanities, Doug Freake, for allowing me to split my sabbatical over two academic years, which provided the opportunity for writing this book in the midst of the other research project. At the time of the initial draft, I was also a Visiting Fellow at the Centre for the Study of Religion and Society of the University of Victoria (although not in residence at the time of writing) and the revisions were done while an Associate Fellow at the Centre. The encouragement of the other fellows and the then director, Harold Coward, were important in carrying this project to completion.

CHAPTER ONE

INTRODUCTION

❖

Who are these creatures called the gods? They are dismissed as idle fictions by atheists and monotheists, capitalists and clergymen alike. But gods, in the plural, are found wherever human beings are found—unless the human beings claim exclusive rights, power and privilege, dispossessing the gods of their homes. Those who ask what a god is, like those who have to ask what a mountain or an eagle or a forest is, will not learn the answer from a book.
—Robert Bringhurst, *A Story As Sharp As a Knife*

Why a Polytheistic Theology?

There are innumerable recordings of myths and stories about the deities, a vast literature of teachings from the goddesses and gods, many works on the rituals and other religious behaviors that relate ourselves to the polytheistic numinous realm, a few philosophical treatises on the logical implications of deities, but no written works that seek systematically to explain the hermeneutics of polytheism in general, rather than within specific cultural traditions. Brief relevant works oriented toward normative Christian culture are beginning to come out of the interrelated African Brazilian and African Caribbean traditions. And there are numerous works on Central African traditions by sympathetic Christians arguing that these traditions are actually monotheistic, a phenomenon to which we shall return later in this book. To the contrary, the monotheistic traditions—the three Religions of the Book (Judaism, Christianity, Islam) and their offshoots—are replete with many works that explain the nature of deity and the impact of this deity on humans.

A recent work (2003) that promises a polytheistic theology, Michael York's *Pagan Theology,* unfortunately does not fulfill its title and exemplifies the problems most Western scholars have in coming to terms with the topic. Divided into three parts, the first part introduces the non-monotheistic traditions of the world under the rubric of "paganism." But it presents these traditions, not from an internal perspective, but from the purview of Western scholars, in the main, presenting these traditions from a Eurocentric perspective, illustrating many of the misunderstandings discussed in chapter 7 of this book. The second part, by far the largest, concerns the religious practices of "paganism" and thus does not directly discuss theology. The third section, "Paganism as Theology," is but a dozen pages in length. Intending to discuss the theology of contemporary Western Neo-paganism it barely touches on the subject, focusing its few pages instead on historical antecedents. Polytheistic theology thus remains an uncharted void in comparative religion.

Given the history of homo sapiens, it may be that polytheism is inherent in human nature, not so much in the sense that it is part of our DNA structure but that it arises from the human experience in conjunction with our nature. For unless we accept the arguments of the ur-monotheists (see chapter 7) that is contrary to the above, monotheism is extremely recent, given the sweep of human history; arose in a tiny part of the planet; and is constantly breaking down.

Monotheism was promulgated by a small number of persons in the eastern Mediterranean region less than three millennia in the past. We know of them because their understanding was privileged in the received version of the Hebrew Bible, but the tone is most often of a single person railing against a polytheistic population. Although the date for the acceptance of

monotheism by a substantial part of this population is contro-
versial, archaeology indicates that it could not have been more
than a few centuries before the end of Israelite religion with the
destruction of the second temple in 70 CE, if then. And it never
was complete. In traditional Judaism, alongside, or within, God,
exists Satan, Lilith, the Shekhina or Matronit, and angels.

Christianity, a development of Hellenized Judaism, understood a single deity in three parts or aspects, developed the
notion of saints as quasi deities, and continued the understanding of angels and Satan. Only certain of the Protestant versions
maintain a relatively strict monotheism. Indeed, until sufficient
Chinese had lived in Christian cultures and gained a better
understanding of Christianity, it was commonly understood in
China that Catholicism and Protestantism were two unrelated
Western religions: the former polytheistic, the primary deity
being the female Mary, and only the latter monotheistic. Similarly, Islam continued the understanding of angels, and in some
Islamic areas, the understanding of saints is important to religious practices. I have recently visited the Hact Bectash shrine in
the town of the same name and the Mevlevi shrine in Konya,
both in central Turkey, and the throngs of pilgrims I encountered
clearly beheld the coffin-enclosed corpses of these revered Sufi
founders as sacred. Similarly, at the old Jewish cemetery in
Prague, I found, based on the fresh pebbles placed upon the
gravestones, that the graves of famous medieval kabbalists are
still visited for their sacred power.

In other words, the monotheistic traditions have constantly
to argue their monotheisms against the human tendency to
relate functionally to multiple numinous entities. Moreover,
Christianity, which constantly divided over, to a non-Christian,
minute differences in theological understandings, developed
ever more complicated creeds that had to be argued. Theology,
along with church politics, was central to these schisms and
became a major feature of the Christian tradition.

So central was theology to Christianity that it is assumed to
be normal to religion. Hence, when Jesuit missionaries entered
China in the late sixteenth century, with a positive attitude
toward Chinese culture and an orientation toward the educated
elite, the lack of theological treatises allowed them to argue that

the educated Chinese were unconscious protomonotheists.
Other Christian missionaries working among the majority of the
population understood the Chinese to be polytheists and, therefore, idolaters and devil worshippers. Yet there was no essential
difference between the religious practices of the elite and ordinary people at that time. In the early twentieth century, sinolo-
gists oriented toward Humanism approvingly took the lack of
theological treatises to mean that the educated Chinese had
always been atheists or, at least, agnostics. They understood that
for well over two thousand years the elite Chinese spent considerable time carrying out sacrificial rituals purely for the sake of
the rituals, with no understanding of recipients of these offerings. In retrospect, this was a rather bizarre interpretation of
Chinese religion.

Similar to the monotheistic traditions, Buddhism, theoretically a nontheistic religion, is also functionally polytheistic.
While the monks and nuns in southern Buddhism may focus on
transcendence through meditation, laypeople seek help from the
Buddha, Arhats, and so on. Northern Buddhism is fully polytheistic, as Buddhas and bodhisattvas are related to as deities. In
any case, Buddhism in Central and East Asia exists within rather
than outside of a larger polytheistic milieu.

What few Westerners seem to realize is the possibility that
polytheism fits the human mind and experience so comfortably
that there is no need for confessional theology per se in polytheistic traditions, especially before they were relatively recently
challenged by the Christian West. Of course, there have been
many thousands of polytheistic cultures, so it is possible that
polytheistic theologies have long been around, and we are
simply unaware of them. Or perhaps it requires someone
coming from a monotheistic background, interested in comparatively analyzing religion, and slowly imbued with polytheistic
understandings and practices, to conceive of doing such a theology. In other words, there is no need of it in polytheistic cultures, but there is a great misunderstanding of these cultures in
monotheistic ones, for Western religions are based on the prem-
ise that polytheists are either inferior human beings or the most
despicable of enemies. Monotheists historically have defined
themselves not positively but negatively, as not being polythe-

ists. Hence, a sympathetic rendering of the hermeneutics of polytheism may be of some value to a hopefully more tolerant contemporary Western civilization in gaining a nonpejorative understanding of non-Western traditions.

A further usefulness of this work may be to assist comparative religionists in understanding polytheistic traditions. Due to the mind-set of singularity normative to monotheistic thinking, it is difficult for beginning Western researchers of polytheistic traditions to understand that in these traditions the numinous are actually multiple. For example, a few years ago I was at an international religious studies conference in South Africa. Several graduate students studying African religions approached me regarding their problems in comprehending the fullness of these traditions. If the rituals are oriented toward the ancestors, then how can Earth, and so on, also be numinous? And what about the deities (who are dead human beings in these traditions)? What needed to be understood is that all of these can be numinous simultaneously, without contradiction and without conflict; this is the essence of polytheism.

Whose Theology?

A confessional theology does not exist in a vacuum. It is a reflection or an argument arising from a person's experience and understanding. Without that link to an individual, it has no meaning; it would be formulaic but not affirmational. If we read Thomas Aquinas's *Summa Theologica*, we are reading the understanding of a known person, with a known background in a specific time and culture. Without that knowledge, the work would lose a fair amount of relevance. Moreover, as polytheism covers all the cultures of the world, save the Religions of the Book, it would be ludicrous to think that any single individual could possibly write a coherent theology that would accurately cover them all, let alone a sufficient number to be properly representative. So I assume that to understand the theology presented here, the reader would need to know enough about the person presenting it to understand the why and how of it, in order to evaluate it.

To put it another way, as my relatives might have said of me as a child, "What is a good Jewish boy doing writing a polytheistic theology?" But I am no longer a boy as I am reaching old age and preparing for retirement and can hardly be said to be religiously Jewish in confessing to being a polytheist, the utter opposite of the simple Jewish creedal statement: "Hear, oh Israel, the Lord your God, the Lord is one!" So how can this be?

The Judaism of my childhood in Baltimore, the period of and just after the Holocaust, was not normative to Judaism as a whole. From my childish perception of the yeshiva and synagogue, it was a Judaism of ritual for its own sake—I perceived no joy, no pleasure in the rituals by the adults around me. But failure to perform the rituals was presented as leading to dire punishment. The God disclosed to me was one who looked for any excuse to punish, but there was no corollary reward. Every year, from Rosh Hashanah to Yom Kippur, we prayed that our sins were not so great that God would have one run over by a streetcar or be given cancer during the coming year. Thus, I could live in fear of God or ignore Him. I chose the latter.

I was already a nontheist before, in my mid-teens, coming across a slim anthology of Buddhist sutra excerpts. The anthology immediately captivated me. It did not simply fill a spiritual void; the early sutras made absolute sense to me, as they seemed to analyze my own experiences. I spent every free moment sitting under an old tree in a quiet part of a large park contemplating the texts. A year later, I was an undergraduate at the University of Chicago and partially neglected the courses in which I was enrolled in order to read each and every book on South Asian religions and other non-Western traditions housed in the University's Divinity School library. I became so thoroughly imbued with the theoretical aspect of Buddhism that its essential epistemology and metaphysics to date remains my own. At that time, the mid-1950s, there were as yet no Buddhist monasteries or meditation centers in North America, quite different from the present-day situation. I considered traveling to Thailand to become a monk but chose mundane life. A Trappist monastery in Iowa, Our Lady of New Mellory, repeatedly allowed me to use its guest quarters for meditation retreats, and

I am still moved by the monks' kindness to an eccentric non-Christian youth.

As an undergraduate, I changed my major yearly, from the premedical course expected of me by my cultural background through biopsychology to psychology (in which I received my degree) to philosophy. In my last year, as a social-science major, I was required to take a year-long course on a non-Western civilization, and by happenstance I ended up taking the course on China rather than India. I was instantly hooked.

My long association with the Divinity School library, where I had been granted the unusual favor of a desk throughout my undergraduate years, led me to enroll in the Divinity School when I graduated. There I was fascinated by Church history; did well in Old Testament studies; poorly in New Testament studies, as I was deemed to have the wrong theological orientation; and, being a nontheist, was utterly bored by theology (entrance examinations exempted me from courses on non-Western religions). Besides, I had entered the Divinity School through the (Unitarian-Universalist) Meadville Theological School (part of the then Federated Theological Faculties) and was, in effect, by the end of my first year kicked out of Meadville for heresy. It was then no place for a non-Christian, and I transferred to the Far Eastern Studies Program of the Oriental Institute, where I was already studying literary Chinese.

Classical Chinese was then taught at Chicago by what was called the "inductive method." This pedagogical theory assumes that language is intimately related to thought processes. One best learned language, not through the study of formal grammar, but by learning to think in the language. It worked for me: not just my thought processes, but my whole perception of reality was transformed. After a couple of years, certain South Asian religious ontological assumptions, such as *saṃsāra,* no longer made any personal sense to me; I was thoroughly imbued with Chinese concrete pragmatism. My worldview shifted to a Buddho-Daoist one, which was more of a subtle than a major change. On completing the language and cultural training of the program, I accepted a fellowship to the new Buddhist Studies program at the University of Wisconsin.

A year of intense Sanskrit and other language studies, along
with the opportunity to study the complex *mādhyamika* philosophy with Edward Conze, left me with the same feeling I had for
Christian theology, and I transferred to the department of Chinese Language and Literature just being formed. That provided
a means for me to begin the first of my residences in Taiwan,
where I had the good fortune to meet and discover a rapport
with some of the last generation to receive a traditional Chinese
education. I became a member, a literally outlandish one, of a
circle of older artists, poets, and connoisseurs. I was culturally,
but not geographically, at home. Chinese identify by culture, not
by race or other criteria, and, given my cultural empathy and
knowledge, I was accepted as Chinese. Over the decades, further stays in Taiwan and the Mainland brought me into contact
and created close relationships with diverse Chinese subcultures, including Chinese Buddhist scholar-monks and Daoist
monk-artists. The last set of relationships I developed was with
the leading members of a new society of spirit-possession mediums. Over a quarter century ago, I married a colleague at a university in Taiwan where I was a visiting professor, and have
since been a member of a large extended Chinese family and a
participant in its family rituals.

At this point, it is necessary to backtrack a bit to explain an
entirely different religious orientation from the above. As a
young child, I lived on the edge of a large park and spent most
of my time there. After World War II, we moved to a new housing development at the then edge of the city, which still had
abandoned rural land on its periphery. Again, I spent much of
my time in this tiny semiwilderness. My parents, to get away
from my rambunctiousness, from the age of eleven sent me to a
distant Boy Scout camp in swampy woods for entire summers. I
remember going to the outdoor chapel the first *shabbas* morning
after I arrived for Jewish services and noticed that my troop
leader, on whom I had developed a crush, was looking up at the
trees and sky during prayers. I asked him about it, and while I
do not remember his words, I recall, in effect, that it was nature
he was worshipping. He had a convert. Not being of the camp's
locale, I was a stranger placed in quarters where everyone else
was from the same troop throughout the year. I spent much of

my time, for three summers, save for the plants and animals, alone in the woods.

In my late teens, for reasons that remain logically inexplicable, I felt compelled to go back to wilderness, alone. Since I was at the University of Chicago, the closest mountains seemed to be the Great Smokies. This was before they became overcrowded. Rather apprehensively I travelled by several buses the longest distance I had ever gone to a place I simply located on a map and, naively, began to hike straight up (there was an easier way elsewhere) the Appalachian Trail to attain the ridge of the Smokies. I ran out of water; I was exhausted (carrying an absurdly heavy and uncomfortable pack based on my late-1940s Boy Scout training and equipment); I was not sure if I was still on the then-faint trail; and I momentarily panicked. After a night's sleep, I recovered, found myself on the mountain's bald top and had a revelation. That mountain was named Mount Thunderhead, surely no accident as I much later learned, and I soon took the name for my first Chinese *hao* (artistic name). From that time, until I moved to a one-room cabin on a small island in central Ontario when I accepted my present position at York University in 1972, I backpacked in various North American wildernesses at least twice a year, never feeling at home until I was over a day's hike from the nearest road.

On the last night of the above-described hike, at a lean-to but a few miles from the road where I would end the trip, another seemingly inconsequential event took place that would prove to have momentous consequences in my life. At that shelter several physically mature local men (I was still a youth) were partying with steaks and beer. They began to entertain themselves by throwing rocks at a bear, perhaps attracted by the smell of their cooking. I still wonder at my untypical courage in stopping them and my success at doing so. The next year I returned to the Smokies to hike the second part of that section of the Appalachian Trail bisected by the highway. A bear walked the trail before me and slept where I did. Within two days, I had extraordinary strength and stamina. I subsequently hiked in a single day what I had planned to take a number of days to do, eating all the food that did not require cooking as I went on, finishing in the early afternoon. Another relationship had been formed that I then also did not understand.

During my first residence in Chinese culture, much as I
enjoyed and admired most facets of it, I came to realize that I
had a home. Being a nonpracticing Jew, I had felt I had no roots.
Repeated experiences of anti-Semitism in the United States, no
spiritual attachment to Israel, and not speaking Yiddish or
having a nostalgic bond to Eastern Europe, from where my
family on both sides had fled from pogroms, left me feeling the
"Wandering Jew." But living in China changed that, for I came
to realize I had a home to which I was emotionally bonded:
North America—not the culture but the land, "Turtle Island."
When I returned, I not only completed my formal Chinese studies, but began to investigate North America's indigenous religions. It seemed to me that the peoples whose homeland was
the land, I now realized, of my own origins and identity would
best know how to relate to it.

As with Chinese culture, my first entry into Native American religious traditions was through the literature (and, as I was
later to realize, this literature was at least, in the main, as grossly
misleading as the literature on Chinese religion). When, after
five years teaching at Indiana State University, I took a position
at York University in Toronto, the situation changed. While
teaching a course that included study of shamanism, a young
Anishnabe, an apprentice shaman, finally could not stand the
nonsensical discussion any longer and broke her silence. We
became each other's mentors and initiated a friendship which
still continues. Years later, I had another long-term Anishnabe
student, also eventually both a friend and mentor, who was then
an apprentice healer. Both profoundly influenced my understanding, introduced me to mature healers, and featured in my
published studies.

Again, as with Chinese culture, I knew that real understanding came from cultural participation rather than books. With my
student and friend, the first mentioned above, I came into contact with a leader of the revitalization of the Midéwewin just
taking place in central Ontario who was willing to serve as my
spiritual guide. I was able to participate in a number of different
rituals over the years, including a series of traditional vision-
questing fasts within a community returning to its spiritual
roots that cemented and enhanced the relationships unwittingly

gained many years before: I was given understandings and shown how to heal for specific needs. I had also begun to assist at a Native way school in Toronto, gaining further traditionalist Native friends and learning by teaching and doing. The school was, for a long time, the center for an urban revitalization and a focus for Native religious leaders passing through. At the urging of my Native friends, eventually I became, in retrospect, too involved, uncomfortably finding myself in the midst of various social, political, and other schisms. Being one of a very few non-Natives at ceremonial gatherings throughout the Great Lakes region, I also found myself perceived by many as a representative of those responsible for all the atrocities done to Native people over the centuries by Euroamericans. It was an identification I could not accept, and after sixteen years of intense participation, increasing racism—a gift of the dominant culture— made me a negative presence at the ceremonies, and I ceased my social but not personal involvement.

After beginning to take part in Native rituals, writing for the first time on the then newly developed personal computer two decades ago, I found myself typing a second conclusion to an article I thought I had finished (on the influences of Christianity on the theology of Native religions). I was not conscious of the words I was typing and eagerly read them as they appeared on the screen. A recent vision-questing fast had led me to the realization of the sex of the spirits that had come to me. One was female, and, to a male brought up in a patriarchal, misogynist religious atmosphere, this had been an epiphany. Now my fingers were adding words beyond the conclusion of what I had thought was a finished article; they were giving reasons for the transition, what I termed the "suppression of female spirituality." This was my first experience of deities overtly directing my actions. Later, this led to a book on comparative female spirituality.

A heightened awareness of practical shamanism, a variety of Native rituals, and the importance of female ritual functions and female spirits led to new perceptions of Chinese religion in these regards on subsequent trips to Taiwan and Mainland China. These interests resulted in my contacting Chinese religious functionaries, including mediums. It also fostered my interest in African Brazilian and African Caribbean forms of mediumism,

which in turn led to an interest in Central-West African religions, which I found to have interesting parallels with early Chinese concepts of kingship and attendant rituals, and so forth.
The involvement with rituals eventually led to my perception of
the power and effects of deities through mediumship, much as I
had earlier encountered it via shamanism. The completion of my
book on female spirituality, the last half finished in two months
when I had expected it to take several more years, I attribute to a
deity who became involved through this mode of relationship
(detailed in chapter 5).

When I first came to Toronto in 1972, where there were a
number of different Buddhist centers, I was invited to meet a
Tibetan lama passing through. At the interview, he immediately
perceived that I was lacking in compassion. He was absolutely
correct. My being imbued with Therevadin and Tantric Buddhist
teachings without direction, even experiencing various modes of
union, including the mystic experience, only reinforced my
understanding of the essential emptiness of everything. As nothing existed, who was there to help and who was there to do the
helping? Native American understandings and practices provided another way, for I learned that one should never do anything for oneself, and the only purpose in life is to help others. It
is, of course, also a Buddhist understanding, but not one I had
imbibed through that tradition, for I had learned without a spiritual mentor. It is the willingness of the deities to assist that
allows me to act in these regards.

These experiences led to a kind of nonpathological schizo-
phrenia. Years ago, when I was leading an advanced class
through a three-hour discussion, a student pointed out to me
that I had just responded oppositely to a query first proposed to
me much earlier in the session. I realized that I had to point out
to the students that they had to let me know from which of my
orientations they wished a response. For my metaphysics
remains Buddho-Daoist, but my functioning may involve my
awareness of spirits, which is predominantly northern Native
North American, while my scholarship is predominantly Western, with an overlay of Chinese pragmatism. These streams of
understanding are not melded into a mishmash but are more in
parallel within my thinking.

Nearly two decades ago, I completed a book on the Native American sacred pipe, which included a brief analysis of its theology. Some reviewers excoriated me for this, basing their criticism on their assumption that Christianity had a monopoly on the use of the term "theology." More recently, I completed a book on comparative female spirituality and realized that the concluding section included a theology of female spirits and a brief theology of polytheism. Increasingly, I came to feel that I should expand this into a more holistic work—hence this study.

All of the above in this section is merely meant to indicate the sources of my understanding. Although my studies have been important, and the experiences of others even more so, I attribute my primary understanding of the deities and spirits, far more than I have indirectly referred to in the preceding, from what they have, both directly and indirectly, imparted to me. For those who will consider this fantasy, the following chapters should be blamed solely on me, not on those with whom I have come into contact.

The Varieties of Polytheism: The Structure of This Book

Given that all but a few of the vast array of religious traditions are polytheistic, albeit the monotheistic ones presently involve a sizable portion of the human population, we would expect to find few if any commonalities. Polytheistic religions do seem to share certain features, however, that contrast them with the monotheistic traditions.

First, the polytheistic traditions are invariably experiential, although this is also true for aspects of each of the Religions of the Book: for example, Hasidism, Pentacostalism, and Sufism. People come to know the deities in polytheistic traditions directly, via such modes as mediumism and shamanism, modes to which we shall return in succeeding chapters. This is one of the reasons for a multiplicity of deities. People with differing personalities and experiences meet differing deities. Without an enforced monotheistic creed, people are open to an abundance of numinous possibilities. Faith is both meaningless and irrelevant. We know what we experience; it takes no leap of faith to assume the reality of deities we have directly encountered. As well, belief is meaningful only in creedal traditions. Without creeds, let alone doctrines, there is nothing requiring explicit belief. Arising from encounters in rituals, visions, and so forth, our acceptance of the validity of the experienced deities is absolutely no different, except more certain, than knowledge gained from sensory experiences.

Second, the relationships with the deities are reciprocal. There are no *prima facie* obligations on either side of the relationships. A deity may come to a person, but usually it is because it was requested. If not, the human need not accept the relationship. If one makes a request of a deity, and especially, if one receives benefits from a deity, it would be gross ingratitude not to make a gesture of appreciation. A deity need not honor a request, in which case the human owes the deity nothing. Indeed, one may then turn to a different deity, who may be more helpful. The current effectiveness of a deity in China can be measured by the condition of the temple in which the deity is the primary focus. The temples are supported by voluntary contributions. If a number of people understand that they have received benefits from the deity, the temple will be in splendid condition due to the many contributions; if people no longer feel these benefits, the temple will be decaying, perhaps collapsing. There are other deities to whom people can turn.

On the other hand, if one creates or accepts a relationship with a deity that has integral obligations, particularly if one makes promises to a deity, then it would be the height of folly to ignore these obligations. We call on deities because they are far more powerful than we are; to deliberately not meet obligations we have made or accepted could be life threatening. This is not because of vengeance but simply due to failure to abide by our promises.

Other than these two important qualities of relationship, the varieties of polytheism are immense. They can, however, be categorized in general from the standpoint of religioecology. That is, the nature of the deities, as well as their functions, tends to reflect the gestalt of a culture's ecological situation with regard to its economy, society, government, terrain, climate, and so on.

All polytheistic traditions recognize in varying ways the various aspects of the cosmos—sun, moon, planets, stars, weather, directions—as deities. For example, many scholars acknowledge that YHWH was a storm deity in incipient Israelite religion. These understandings will be the focus of chapter 2.

For most of human history, we humans lived intimately with nature. Whether gathering, gardening, hunting, or fishing, we knew we were dependant on animals and plants to give their lives to us so that we could live. Chapter 3 will be concerned with animal, plant, and mineral (stones and metals) spirits and their relationship with humans. In these traditions, shamanism was often the means of interacting with the spirit realm for the benefit of one's family and community.

As gardening became important, we began to be more sedentary, living for extended periods of time in a single locale. Our family dead remained with us and became a source of spiritual power. We communicated with them by allowing our bodies to be their temporary abodes while they directly communicated with the living. Ancestral and related spirits are the focus of chapter 4.

On the model of the family dead being spirits essential to the well-being of the living, the dead of nonfamily slowly became important: ghosts may become deities and, in turn, the deities become anthropomorphic. Mediumism remains the most common mode of interaction. Chapter 5 is concerned with these types of deities and means of communication with them.

There are other deities or semideities (the offspring of deities and humans) who are important to human cultures both by their talents or gifts to us and by the example of their lives. In the literature, they are often termed "culture heroes" or "tricksters." Rarely are rituals directed toward them, but they are most important in myths, particularly those concerned with the recreation of the world (as compared with the monotheistic focus on original creation). Chapter 6 will discuss these types of deities.

The monotheistic traditions are poorly prepared to understand polytheistic ones. Not only are the understandings of the Religions of the Book utterly at variance with the actualities of polytheism, but those of Western traditions trying to understand it are often wide of the mark due to their ethnocentrisms. Typical monotheistic misperceptions of polytheism are the subject of chapter 7, as well as the effects on polytheistic

religious traditions of domination by monotheistic ones consequent to colonialism.

What then are the hermeneutics of polytheism in general?
What does it mean to be human with these understandings? The
last chapter will explore meanings from the standpoint of
selected lifestyles and rituals.

A Few Caveats

In this work, I am using the term "theology" in its literal
sense: "to speak of the deities." Technically, I should use the split
term "thea/theology," since, of course, I am discussing both
female and male divinities. Such a term is most awkward. So I
hope I will be forgiven for using "theology" in a more inclusive
sense than the Greek origin would imply.

There are many types of theological discourses. Chapters
2–6 encompass a form of systematic theology in that they systematically delineate many of the different types of deities found
in polytheistic religions. Chapters 7–8 involve a mode of comparative theology, but not in the sense of comparing different
polytheistic theologies. Rather the comparison is solely between
monotheism and polytheism in general. In this work, the term
"confessional theology" is used. Most often the term refers to
the theology of a particular Christian confession, in the sense of
a creedal formulation. Here, the term is being used in another
sense, as the "confession" of an individual's—my own—system
of theological understanding

When appropriate, as this is a confessional theology, I will
relate pertinent experiences and understandings to help eluci-
date the points being made. Both Native American and Chinese
teachings emphasize reticence in these regards. From the former
perspective, one may not reveal the contents of one's visions or
name those numinous beings to whom one is connected, save to
the elder guiding one if young or a neophyte, unless the vision
is for a group. To do so violates one's relationship, leading to
loss of the power inherent in the vision. It is not that one keeps
one's relationships secret, but they are revealed indirectly
through symbols, songs given by the spirits, stories, and so on.
Those who understand and need to know will know. It is only

when one reaches my present age that it is considered proper for one who has some understanding to speak of these matters. Perhaps this is because with age and, hopefully, a modicum of wisdom, one has learned just what to reveal and the right reasons for revealing it. Chinese teachings emphasize that those who are aware of these matters normally keep silent; those who are voluble in these regards are not to be trusted to know anything. Hence, I will ask you, the reader, to bear with me when I am oblique and limit what I reveal to the bare essential minimum.

Finally, it is crucial that the reader understand the point made about voice. One meaning of "theology" is to theorize from within a particular tradition, but the opposite is being done here. In any case, polytheism is not a specific tradition; the term merely labels what it is not. That is, polytheism is not monotheism. The understandings expressed here represent the thinking of only a single individual, and an anomalous one at that. Humans are social beings and normally function within specific communities. My community, for nearly a half century, has been that of modern international Western scholarship. I speak from that tradition, as critical as I am of it, and none other; no other tradition, no other community is represented here. While there will be many references to Native American and Chinese traditions, some reference to African, African Brazilian, circumpolar, and Polynesian cultures, as well as mention of the Religions of the Book and Buddhism, no statement here should be understood as representing these traditions. Only persons from within these traditions can speak for them theologically. In summary, I am but professing my own individual perceptions and interpretations, based on my experiences within certain polytheistic traditions, for whatever use that may be to others.

CHAPTER TWO

THE COSMIC COUPLE: MOTHER EARTH AND FATHER SKY

❖

He then turns the stem of it towards the heavens, after this towards the earth, and now holding it horizontally moves himself around until he has completed a circle.

—Jonathan Carver describing the Native use of the sacred pipe in the northern Mississippi area in the mid-eighteenth century, quoted in Paper, *Offering Smoke*

Sky and Earth

We are all terrestrial creatures. Save for cave mouths and rock shelters, or floating platforms tethered to the shore, we live on the ground. We may venture into deep caves or risk our lives on ocean voyages, but we cannot fly without highly complex technology. We may swim until exhausted, but again, we cannot venture below the water's surface, except for a few minutes, without intricate machinery. We feel comfortable on the ground and, until it was paved over, as children we thrilled to the feel of the dust between our toes or playing with and in mud. For most of our history, we slept on the dirt, perhaps cushioned by a thin layer of leaves or animal skins. We rested on Earth as on the bosom of our mother.

Until we polluted the lakes and streams, we sipped the water, our lives utterly dependant on it, as we sucked the milk from our mothers' breasts. (The relatively recent massive pollution of the waters may well correlate with the unnatural practice of bottle nursing.) The food we require for life either grows directly from the soil or the waters or else consists of herbivores and omnivores who eat plant life and whom we eat in turn. Earth nurses us and feeds us as do our mothers, who themselves in turn are dependant on Earth.

Above us is an entity on which we also depend. It contains a bright disk, so bright we cannot look directly at it if the sky is clear, that both warms us and lights the world around us. Not only are we dependant on Sun for life, but the plants on which we also depend require sunlight for growth. From above falls the rain on which our ultimate food, plant life, is also dependant. We rely on Sky as we do Earth.

But Sky has a different temperament from Earth. Save for the very occasional earthquake and volcanic eruption, Earth is benign; we do far more harm to Her than She has ever done to us. Sky is different; His power is hardly subtle. Sun warms us, but too much of Him can burn us, can literally bake our brains, yet an insufficient amount means we starve. Rain is part of Storm, whose lightening, if we are the highest object around, can kill us. Too much rain and we can drown; too little, and again we starve. These variations are hardly rare, although severe aspects are uncommon. We humans tend to relate to Earth with great affection; to Sky, with awe and trepidation.

Humans, from their very beginnings, noted the parallel between male mammals ejaculating fertilizing liquid into females to begin new life and the falling of rain from Sky and its absorption by Earth for plants to germinate. It may be necessary to interject at this point a response to the still common modern Western conceit that the physical roles of males and females in the creation of life was discovered by early modern Western civilization. Any gardener or farmer certainly knows the relationship as does anyone dependant on hunting for survival. The cave paintings that date back to the earliest humans provide evidence of that understanding even then. What they did not have, of course, was the Victorian era's horror of the human body and its workings.

Since we live between Earth and Sky, since our lives are utterly dependant on their conjoining, it is natural for us to conceive of Earth and Sky as our parents. It is equally natural, given their very natures and how they affect us, that most cultures understand Earth, or Sea for maritime peoples, as our mother and Sky as our father (exceptions include early Egypt, which reversed this sexual identification of Earth and Sky). Virtually every culture save one, for which we have some awareness, has so understood and related to Earth. The sole exception is the interrelated monotheistic complex, and even this understanding ultimately derives from this acknowledgment of our cosmic parents. For many scholars of the Hebrew Bible understand YHWH to have been originally a storm deity, and for most, if not all of Israelite history, He had a spouse who was Earth (or Sea for the Canaanites), Asherah, whose image was not only in the Temple but in virtually every household. From a negative perspective, one could argue that monotheism arises from an antifemale aberration, from the excision of the Mother from the divine couple, leaving but the Father to reign in lonely and unnatural magnificence.

Most cultures understand creation of every sort to be due to the sexual pairing of equal, complementary deities. For instance, the Polynesian Maori of present-day New Zealand understood the primal parents to be Papa, the Earth mother, and Rangi, the Sky father. From the primal parents were born humans, forests, undomesticated and domesticated plants, oceans, and storms. In cultures where precedence is given to one of the pair, it is invariably the female partner. For it is the female who gestates, births, and nurtures new life; the essential male role is brief and other roles are tangential. In the rare case of parthenogenesis, the male is not even necessary.

Again most cultures conceive of humans as reflecting this primal coupling. Our bodies are often conceived as formed from the soil (dust, mud, clay) of Earth and our life (vital energy) from the breath (wind) of Sky. In cultures where irrigation was necessarily developed early, the waters may be perceived as the male fertilizing, vitalizing substance. In either scenario, we humans are composed of earth and water. In the more complex formulations of developed civilizations, there are variations. In China, it is understood that our form or material bodies come from the pairing of Sky and Earth and our vital energy from the interrelationship of Yin and Yang (opposing elemental forces, including, respectively, female and male).

Hence, every culture, given the monotheistic exception, celebrates and offers thanks to the divine pair, from a simple acknowledgment of the first of a set of offerings to the magnificent rituals of complex civilizations. Even chimpanzees have been observed to dance ritually in the presence of thunderstorms and waterfalls, and these are the only circumstances in which this behavior has been noted. As examples, two very different sets of rituals demonstrate the variety of ways in which humans acknowledge the cosmic couple.

Circumpolar Rebirth Rituals

Throughout the subpolar regions, there are rituals that involve intense heat in an enclosed space. In both Eurasia and the Americas, these rituals diffused southward well into the temperate regions. In areas that became monotheistic, they have become secularized. Thus, from Scandinavia through eastern Europe into the Islamic Mediterranean and, earlier, in the Roman world, saunas and steam baths are common. In the Native cultures of the Americas, we can still find their original religious import.

In the Americas, from the northern Anishnabe cultures through the Missouri, Mississippi, and Ohio valleys down to the Mayan of southern Mesoamerica, there is a remarkable commonality of ritual practices and understandings, even though the structures may vary from the covered wigwams of skin, bark, or now canvas, through small caves cut into river banks, to the complex stone structures of the Mayans. Even more remarkable, until recently, has been the failure of Euroamericans to understand these rituals as other than a secularized bath. Hence, the Western term for these rituals: "sweat lodge." (The equivalent would be calling Christian churches "dressing-up lodges.") This is not simply the case of the literature of the past, but of well-known scholars of Native American religions who have limited observation experience but have never themselves participated. On the other hand, anyone who has participated, including Christian clergy, has invariably been struck by the intense spirituality of the experience.

To respect the esoteric nature of Native religious rituals, the following description of the "spirit lodge," as the ritual is termed in some northern Native languages, is generalized from a number of contiguous northern Native traditions speaking Algonkian and Siouan languages. No details of any single tradition will be delineated.

A structure barely large enough to hold the expected number of participants is constructed with a skeleton of flexible branches, preferably from trees that grow along the water, such as willow, to symbolize Earth's gift of water to us. One end of these branches is placed in a hole in the ground and the other end is tied to a corresponding branch on the other side of the circle of branches. A second set of branches is tied horizontally around the poles, leaving a small opening on the side facing east (or west or south, depending on the cultural tradition). These poles and branches are used in multiples of four, the sacred number. A pit is dug in the center of the circle. Earth from this pit is often then used to create an altar a short distance from the opening, the space between the two especially sacred. The framework was originally covered with hides or bark, but now canvas, quilts, blankets, anything at hand is used to create a light-tight structure. (Plastic tarps are now also used but are possibly dangerous as they are totally impermeable to air exchange.) Except for the pit, the ground is covered with sacred fragrant plants, such as cedar leaves or sage (not sagebrush, which is an import). A short distance from and facing the opening, which will be covered by flaps in the coverings during the ritual, a fire is built, with a particular pattern of logs, inside of which are rocks that will nor crack on heating (exploding rocks being dangerous).

Every item used in the structure, fire, and ceremony is gathered ritually; that is, every item is spoken to, asked if it is willing to be used by humans in the ritual and told why it is important to humans, and offered a sacred substance, usually tobacco. For every aspect of the structure, every item used, is, in itself, numinous, an individual sacred entity, with a will and power of its own. It is this power that humans are requesting for their needs; hence, these items must offer themselves willingly and these offerings must be reciprocated.

During the building of the structure, the altar, and the fire, the women and men have specific, differing roles. When the structure is completed and the rocks are heated, usually after dusk, male or female participants strip themselves completely to enter the lodge as they entered the world (males and females did not traditionally, except perhaps as families, participate in the same heat ritual). Now, given the adoption of European prudery, younger male Natives tend to wear bathing suits or wrap towels around themselves and females wear body-covering garb in the lodge. Before entering, the participants offer tobacco and purifying herbs to the spirits via the sacred fire and are purified with the smoke of specific herbs: sweetgrass, cedar, or sage (elsewhere, other substances are used, such as sweet pine and copal). All movement follows the path of the sun around the lodge and fire. Except for those attending the fire who will not enter the lodge, no one crosses between the fire and the lodge opening, often marked by a line of cedar or sage leaves. The opening is deliberately low and one must crawl to enter.

After all have been purified, made their offerings, and crawled into the lodge and are sitting knee to knee, shoulder to shoulder, in the cramped space surrounding the pit, the rocks, now red-hot, are maneuvered in by the fire tender(s). They are individually greeted by the participants and placed in the pit. After the ritually proper number of rocks have been brought in, the flaps are closed and made light tight, water is sprinkled on the rocks, and the lodge is filled with live steam and increasing heat. The participants begin to chant, speak, or pray, depending on the particular tradition or individual ritual leaders.

After awhile, the flaps are opened to allow the participants a breathe of fresh air and are soon closed again. Often this goes on for four rounds. When the ritual is completed, the perspiration-soaked participants crawl out on the ground and introduce themselves to all who may have gathered around the lodge to lend the participants their support. If there is a stream, lake, or spring nearby, they will plunge in; if not, they will dress.

Such are the outlines of the ritual; they tell us nothing of the meaning nor of the experiences that people have. It is the hermeneutics of the ritual that can provide a glimpse as to why this is invariably a profound spiritual experience and why, among the oldest of human rituals, it persists to today.

The ground of Earth itself, the branches of willow or similar trees that indicate the streams that are the blood of Earth, the skin or bark coverings that are the gifts of Earth together create a cavelike atmosphere, and in some traditions people dig small caves along the banks of streams for this purpose. We now know that the earliest humans performed religious rituals in the dark recesses of caves. It becomes a womb of Earth and the pit is Her uterus. Facing this womb is a bright fire, the earthly representative of Grandfather Sun, itself representing Sky. Out of this fire come rocks blazing red as the early morning or evening sun. Although originally of the feminine Earth, they have been transformed by the masculine Fire and now are of the essence of Sun and Sky. Greeted as Grandfathers, the male sacred persons, they are placed in Earth's uterus and provide the only light in the lodge.

The hot rocks are sprinkled with water, connoting the life-giving rain and semen, and live steam permeates the structure. When the Grandfathers are placed in the pit, Earth's uterus, in the darkness, the lodge representing the canopy of the dark night, the female Sky, cosmogony is recapitulated. Male Sky has entered female Earth; it is an act of cosmic coition and the life force is generated. The entire cosmos and all inside are reconceived, can start life anew. It is a time out of time, a space out of space. In the agonizing pain of primal chaos and rebirth, we become one with the cosmos. We are very, very close to the most potent of spiritual energies and are absorbed by it. Our bodies feel the powers and are nearly overwhelmed. When we leave the lodge, crawling through the opening, Earth's vagina, along the line of cedar leaves that is the umbilical cord, we are wet, hot, red, and in discomfort. No different from the newborn, we are truly reborn. Hence, we must introduce ourselves to those around us, for they are meeting us for the very first time.

But this is not all. In the lodge, the intense heat causes massive perspiration, leading to dehydration. The increased metabolism of the participants in the small sealed structure reduces the oxygen and increases carbon dioxide, causing hypoxyventilation. The darkness engenders partial sensory deprivation. The near-scalding steam and hours spent cramped in the tightly confined space are most uncomfortable, perhaps causing the production of endorphins. Drumming and chanting with the use of shakers (rattles) may lead to auditory driving. Awareness of the symbolic and mythic nature of our immediate surroundings makes us especially sensitive to the entry of numinous beings. In summary, any of these effects may engender shamanic trance; combined, they readily lead to a light trance.

The intense communality, heightened by our bodies being pressed against each other, with a totally shared experience, means that an individual's trance experience may become that of the group as a whole. We share our lives and our relationship with particular spirits; we become a spiritual brotherhood or sisterhood with all present. Hence, this ritual is a common preliminary for the ritual leaders of more complex ceremonies. This bonding and regeneration allows trouble-free planning and interacting. We make our prayers public. And we confess to our sisters or brothers; we purge ourselves of our pain, shame, grief, and misery. Many cry. This purging too is essential for a spiritual rebirth. We can become new persons only by evacuating old ills. Thus, this ritual is also commonly done for healing.

Hence, the ritual has manifold functions. It is a preliminary to others; it is used for healing; it is used at times of stress; and it is used simply when a need is felt for renewal, for intensely contacting the numinous realm and becoming reenergized from the experience. It is as fulfilling as a ritual can be, in part because it brings us into physical and spiritual contact not only with Earth and Sky, but in their glorious and mysterious life-creating interaction.

Chinese Imperial Sacrifices to Sky and Earth

Fundamental to Chinese religion from its inception in the distant Neolithic past is the offering and sharing of food with the family dead, to be discussed in chapter 4. But associated with this basic ritual are offerings to cosmic and nature spirits. The most important of these latter rituals is the offering to Sky and Earth.

Over the course of millennia, Earth came to be conceived in a variety of modes. For farmers, she is a divine couple, Grandmother and Grandfather Earth, representing the union of male and female essential to fertility. As an abode of the corpse and that soul, of the two human souls, which remains with it, Earth is an official of the underworld bureaucracy and, accordingly, male; prior to the full emergence of the bureaucratic mentality, she was female in this guise as well. For merchants, Earth is one of the mercantile deities and also male. In villages and towns, there will be a small temple to the protector of the locality, the Lord of Place. Often a famous general or magistrate of the past, if the protector proves ineffectual, he can be replaced by another. For others, she is a single female deity. All made offerings to Earth for this multiplicity of reasons.

But the most important aspect of Earth is being half of the generative pair *tiendi* (Sky-Earth). Philosophically, it was understood that humans, as well as all existing things, receive their form, their material aspect, from the conjoining of Sky and Earth and their energy, their life force, from the interaction of Yin and Yang. Sky and Earth are the parents of us all.

Before the political unification of the Chinese empire, some twenty-two hundred years ago, especially when there was a semifeudal system, lesser rulers made offerings to a female deity of Soil and Grain, both for continued agricultural fertility and in recognition of their suzerainty over a specific territory. The superior ruler alone made offerings to the supreme cosmic couple, *tiendi*. This became both the prerogative and primary responsibility of the emperor and his spouse; for anyone else to do so was ipso facto treason. Hence, the emperor and his spouse were called the Father and Mother of the People, for, among other reasons, they alone made offerings to the cosmic Mother and Father.

For much of Chinese history, the two were worshipped together at a single altar. In the fifteenth century, to create a more magnificent array of altars, the two were separated. North of the imperial palace was the Altar to Earth; south was

the Altar to Sky. East of the palace was the Altar to Sun; west
the Altar to Moon. Related was the Altar to Soil and Grain
(female) on the west of the grand entrance to the palace, bal-
anced by the Imperial Clan Temple (patrilineal/male) on the
east side of the entrance.

The altars to Sky and Earth consist of three levels, each
smaller than the one below, round for Sky and square for Earth,
following Chinese symbolism. They are unenclosed, although
the enormous grounds in which they are found are walled. The
Altar to Sky is of white marble; the Altar to Earth, of plain soil.
Near them are large, magnificent structures for the preparation
of the ceremonies. On the day preceding the sacrificial offerings,
the emperor and hundreds of his retinue, including musicians
and those who assist in the ritual, richly robed, make a grand
procession to the respective altar. The emperor retires to the
main preparation building, where he purifies himself and men-
tally prepares for this most sacred of his activities, the one that
justifies his political superiority. On the day of the sacrifice, complex rituals take place, but the offerings are made by the
emperor himself,

Simultaneously, in the palace, the empress carries out identical rituals, for, following Chinese custom, the male carries out the
rituals outside of the residence, and the female, inside, indicating
the original warrior aspect of the sociopolitical roles. Western
writings on these rituals not only ignore the offerings to Earth,
but the empress's ritual roles as well—female sacrality, save for
virgin females, is inconceivable in the monotheistic traditions.
These rituals ended with the collapse of imperial rule in 1911, but
these altars can still be found in Beijing as public parks.

Sun and Moon

The cosmic couple is not limited to Earth and Sky, but tend
to be conceived in various cosmic pairings, sometimes married
siblings, varying from culture to culture: Sun and Earth, Thunderstorm and Earth, Sun and Moon, Morning Star and Evening
Star, Day Sky and Night Sky. As discussed above, Sun and
Thunderstorm are the most potent of Sky phenomena as they
affect our planet's inhabitants. With Earth is associated dark-

ness, as found in deep caves. And human females not only follow Earth's pattern in bringing forth life but emulate (actually are physically influenced by) the exact timing and rhythm of Moon in their estrous cycles, intimately related to their fertility.

With Sun the focus of the day and darkness and Moon that of night, their association with Sky and Earth is assured. While we cannot stare at the unclouded Sun without unshaded eyes, we can at Moon. She lights our way in the darkness; Her comfort and beauty are readily accessible. As a modern male, even though I know the moon also to be a huge rock on which humans, with great technological effort, can walk, I still address Her, with considerable affection and a lump in my throat, as Grandmother every time I meet Her. And I can only contemplate with wonder how the Native traditionalist women I know must feel about Her, given that they bond with Her every moon cycle for much of their lives.

Throughout the Incan empire, Sun and Moon were the divine couple (although the Inca also recognized *pachamama*, Mama Earth), represented in the world by the ruling couple, usually brother and sister, who were also husband and wife. The male Inca, as the Sun, made offerings at the Temple of the Sun, full of gold (the sweat of Sun) images, where his mummified male ancestors were housed. The female Inca, as the Moon, made offering at the corresponding Temple of the Moon, full of silver (the tears of Moon) images, where her mummified female ancestors were placed.

But there are exceptions to this pattern, particularly in the polar regions, where the sex of Sun and Moon tend to be understood as opposite to that in temperate climes. As Louis Bäckman, a Saami scholar, related to me from her own experiences, after the winter darkness, Sun first appears as a golden glow on the mountains. Daily, the glow becomes more intense and beautiful. The appearance of the Sun, low on the horizon, brings joy to Arctic peoples. In contrast, during the winter darkness, Moon remains high in the sky, shining with a bright, cold light, creating a feeling of dread. For much of the year, Sun remains low on the horizon, close to Earth; it is Moon that rides high in the sky. Hence, in this part of the world, Sun tends to be understood as female and Moon as male.

Recently, I had the opportunity to travel to the high Arctic, around the latitude of 75°, close to the time of the autumn equinox. It was not long before I felt that I was on a different planet. This was not the sky I knew. The sun at midday was at the height it would be in the temperate zone in late afternoon, and at midnight, it was as light as an hour after sunset in the temperate zone. While the larger planets could be seen, the stars could not, as there was too much light. The moon was higher than the sun when visible, and I could imagine how baleful that light could appear during the long Arctic winter night. Most unnerving of all to an inhabitant of the temperate zone was that the sun always appeared to be to the north! Hence, it is far from surprising that the Inuit cosmic concepts differ from those of most cultures. It is interesting to speculate whether the Japanese understanding of Amaterasu, the Sun, as female is due to diffusion from the Arctic.

Similarly, those inhabiting arid regions would also have differing cosmic concepts. For example, before the building of the Aswan Dam, the major source of water for agriculture in Egypt was the annual flooding of the Nile. That river replaced rain as the primal source of fertility; hence, in early Egypt, it was conceived as male and Sun as female. Other cosmic entities similarly had different gender connotations from most other cultures.

The Four Directions

We humans tend to understand our world as bisected by the east-west line of Sun's path, crossed by a north-south perpendicular. Christians often misunderstood the common symbol of this understanding, an equal-armed cross, as proto-Christian, representing the cross of Roman criminal execution and the risen Christ rather than the world. (Since the actual Roman execution device was T-shaped, the misrepresentation in Christian symbolism of a cross for this device may be due to the commonality of the cross symbolizing the world.) In China, there is frequent reference to the "Four Quarters," and, as described above, the altars to the cosmos were arranged according to these directions. In the Spirit Lodge described above, it is understood that there are four entrances, one for each of the directions, although but one is physically open, by which the spirits may enter.

In northern Native American traditions, the Four Directions, or Four Winds, as they are also known, are each deities in and of themselves. Various symbols are connected to them, such as colors, animals, plants, and so on, varying from culture to culture, clan to clan. Given the rotation of the Earth, winds generally come from the west, bringing storms with them. Hence, West Wind is often also associated with the Thunders. He is male, powerful, and potentially dangerous, but also necessary to our lives. As Thunder, he is frequently conceived as an enormous bird, the Thunderbird, shooting forth lightening. Those who are connected to thunder power often, but not necessarily, meet and speak with him in his bird form.

East and West, as the path of Sun, also represent the path of life, from birth with the rising sun to death with the setting sun. Hence, it is West, at its furthest extreme, that is perceived as the abode of the dead, and corpses are placed facing west. Similarly in China, the abode of the dead has been amalgamated with the Buddhist Pure Land, forming the Western Paradise as the ideal locale for one's family dead. But, in Native traditions, the cycle of life can also be represented by all Four Directions corresponding to the four seasons: from birth through childhood in the East, to adolescence and early maturity in the South, to late maturity in the West, to old age and death in the North. For those living in temperate climes of the northern hemisphere, South means growth and nurture, while North is cold and foreboding, although it may be a congenial source of power for those with such a connection.

Ubiquitous to Native North American traditions is the making of offerings to the Four Directions, Sky, and Earth (the order will vary). This is especially the case for tobacco offerings, whether offered directly or as smoke. Some traditions, perhaps influenced by the Western importance of the number seven, add a seventh offering, to all the beings, the subject of the next chapter. Such patterns of offering acknowledge the entirety of the cosmos and place one intimately in contact with the numinous universe as a whole.

Morning Star / Evening Star

Another common cosmic pairing is that of Evening and Morning Stars. The male Morning Star is associated with the day, with beginnings, with the Sun. Female Evening Star relates to night, to endings, Moon, and Stars. Often they are perceived as brother and sister.

Sun and Earth

Similarly, rather than the couple of Sky and Earth, the cosmic couple may be seen as Sun and Earth. Sun travels across the sky, entering Earth at the distant western horizon, where He couples with Earth, until He rises in the morning in the east to begin his journey again. (In ancient Egypt, Sun enters Sky's mouth and emerges from Her vagina each morning.)

Stars and Planets

Of course, as Morning and Evening Stars, various stars, individually and in clusters or constellations, as well as the other planets, are understood by virtually all cultures to be numinous. Here, the many understandings are so varied and complex that generalizations are difficult, if not impossible, and best avoided.

Mountains and Streams

Chinese kings and, later, emperors made offerings to cosmic and nature deities other than Sky-Earth. Beside the main road leading to the Imperial Palace across from the Altar to Sky are a complex of imperial altars, including a set to the Earth Spirits and the Sky Spirits. The former houses altars to the Four Mountains and the Four Seas; the latter, altars to Wind, Clouds, Rain, and Thunder. Every Chinese emperor and the earlier kings, including legendary ones, made offerings at the top of Mount Tai ("The Great Mountain") and also directly to the Huangho ("The Yellow River").

When I first began writing on this topic with regard to China a number of years ago, I confused the Chinese linguistic predilection for binomial expressions with a complementary, oppositional pair. Imbued with the unconscious penchant towards Freudian interpretations that is typical of modern Western intellectuals, I understood the Chinese expression *shanshui* ("Mountains and Streams," usually and incorrectly translated as "landscape") to stand for the male and female aspects of nature. It was only later, when I was mapping out the locations of the imperial altars in Beijing and coming across Chinese poetic ruminations on the term, that it became apparent to me that Mountains and Streams meant Earth alone, mountains indicating the solid aspect of Earth and streams the liquid aspect. It is difficult to rid ourselves, as modern educated Westerners, of Freud's pathetically juvenile obsession that anything tall represents a penis.

In North America I have hiked up, and occasionally climbed, many mountains and am hardly unique in finding the experience spiritual. But I have also been fortunate to have the opportunity to ascend the two most sacred mountains in China: Mount Tai and Mount Lu. The former, the highest place in northeastern China, arising from a flat plain, contains one temple after another along the route to the top (and there were more in the past) and major temples at its summit (to the anthropomorphized deities of the mountain). The thousands of years as a center for ritual activities leave an enormous sacred aura that is palpable. Many tens of thousands of pilgrims and tourists continue to ascend it each and every day.

Mount Lu, in the center of China, on the south shore of the Yangtze River, sacred to both Buddhists and Daoists and featured in Chinese poetry and paintings for nearly two millennia, is another matter. Christian missionaries decided to use it for a summer resort in the late nineteenth century and, under the protection of Western armies and gunboats on the nearby Yangtze River, tore down every one of the many temples on its summit and slopes. All that remains, aside from Christian churches built from the stones of the Buddhist and Daoist temples, are sacred groves and caves where temples once stood. On the vast expanse of its summit, the major feeling is of desecration.

Again, the seas and rivers fascinate us regardless of cultural background—else why are seashores favorite resorts everywhere? I grew up in an East Coast North American seaport; felt a need to go to sea as a youth; fortunately had the opportunity to sail the Atlantic and Caribbean in the now barely existing United States Merchant Marine; spent most of my life along the shores of the Great Lakes; and have recently moved to the West Coast, on the shore of the Strait of Juan de Fuca, in anticipation of retirement. In Rio de Janeiro, hundreds of thousands throng the shoreline on the day for making offerings to the Sea Goddess.

The focus of Chinese religio-aesthetics is *shanshui*, and outside of China, the mistranslated "landscape" is probably the best known aspect of Chinese art, aside from its pottery (which is but shaped earth). These paintings are iconographic; they are meant to bring the numinous Earth into the interior of homes, to make available a means of contemplating Her when separated from Her by the urban environment.

Native Americans also, of course, had sacred mountains and waters. Euroamericans constantly seek to wrest these away from them. Perhaps the epitome of this continued desacralization is Devil's Tower National Monument, the Native name of which translates to Bear Lodge. The American National Park Service perpetuates the Christian missionary understanding of Native American deities, such as Bear, to be the Devil. Another popular sacred vision-questing site in the northern plains of the United States is Bear Butte, in the sacred Black Hills, which has been turned into a state park, so that tourists can gawk at fasting Natives. Natives are still fighting losing battles to protect their sacred lakes and rivers, such as Blue Lake and the Oldman (Coyote) River.

Personal Relationships with Cosmic Powers

Personal relations with cosmic forces are not only possible but far from unusual. Relations with the beings discussed in the next chapter may include their linkages with one of the Directions or the cosmic couple. These understandings, based on personal visions, potentially differ from one person to another. My relationship with the numinous animal mentioned in chapter 1, closely linked, as we shall see, with the Earth Mother, eventually led me to direct involvement with Her. The most important of these events, those which are to be shared, are detailed in two places in my book, *Through the Earth Darkly: Female Spirituality in Comparative Perspective*. These events have left me with an overwhelming warm feeling of belonging "here," of connectedness, and of the utter naturalness of being supported and nurtured by Earth.

The relationship with the first numinous entity mentioned in the previous chapter developed earlier and is far different. When I had moved to a small island in central Ontario in 1972, I began a ritual relationship. I was then untutored and feeling my way; only a few years later would I have the opportunity to learn how to do these things properly, in the tried and tested manner of a long established tradition. I had not at first learned that one does not develop such a relationship lightly. Two years later, with a new infant, our first, and all the complications that entails, I neglected to carry out a major ritual I had initiated. That day, in late autumn, I closed up the cabin and took a load of baggage, crib, and so forth, in a steel utility boat for the short five-minute trip to where I docked and left my wife and baby behind for the second trip. Suddenly, I found myself pushed by enormous westerly wind-driven waves, not present when I left my dock seconds earlier, in a small bay that was invariably calm, onto the top of a low bridge. It took hours, with the help of neighbors, to get the heavy boat off, face it into the gale and return. When I did so, I found a ring of toppled trees encircling the cabin, but the cabin and those inside were safe and undamaged. Needless to say, the next time I carried out the ritual, I did so, in Kierkegaard's terms, literally in "fear and trembling." And I have never since failed in the obligation I took on; nor has the spirit failed me, even when on the other side of the planet, to my great surprise. It was a most powerful lesson. Later I was to learn that in Native traditions, it was assumed that when one made a vow to the spirits, particularly cosmic ones, one's life and that of one's family became the collateral.

In the most important vision I received when fasting, I was taught how to use ritual paraphernalia that I had previously been given by several sources to heal by bringing together selected energies of the cosmic pair, to join together what we modern humans had separated. What I subsequently understood, as I watched the words form on the computer screen, in the event described in chapter 1, was that I was also being directed to heal in a larger sense. I was to attempt to bring to the attention of a culture gone patriarchally mad the great loss engendered by utterly ignoring female spirituality. For the last sixteen years, this increasingly became the focus of my research and writing. My previous book, mentioned above, focused on what had been lost in Western traditions; this work is more holistic, as it concerns both male and female spiritual essences and their interrelationships.

CHAPTER THREE

NUMINOUS NATURE: ANIMAL, PLANT, AND MINERAL SPIRITS

❖

When you hear a twig snap on the edge of the garden, you shouldn't look in that direction because it's the manioc mother. If you look at her, she gets angry and shits weeds. The whole garden fills with weeds. If you don't look at her, she is happy. She shits manioc and the plants grow quickly.

—Saying of the Aguaruna women of the Amazonian forest in Michael E. Brown, *Tsewa's Gift*

Introduction

For most of human existence, our habitations did not separate us from nature. A skin or bark lodge cover, a woven leaf or mud-daubed reed hut, or a branch-covered pit dwelling allowed the sounds of passing animals, of trees and shrubs moving in the wind, or the patter of a drizzle to be heard. Daily, we learned the movements of animals in their tiniest details and the life cycles of a great variety of plants. Our lives were utterly dependant on the weather, on animals, and on plants; they, in turn, were not dependant on us.

37

As we all are both individuals and representative of the human species, so we understood the plants and animals with which we came into contact. Just as we would eventually learn how distant people treated our kin and sometime in the future might have the opportunity to interact with them accordingly, so we knew that how we treated plants and animals would effect not just the being before us, but, in time, how every member of the species might relate to us. Even more important, we needed their lives to live. We needed plants and animals to sacrifice their own lives in support of our own. Why should they do this?

We realized that to catch an unwilling animal was difficult; far better were it to offer itself. We learned to communicate with animals and plants, to ask them to share their lives with us. All we could offer in turn was respect and reverence for their sacrifice. We developed rituals in these regards: to speak to the animals or plants, point out our need and beg them to take pity on us, to offer token sacred substances to them as a gesture of reciprocity; to never waste their gift of their lives; to honor them in ceremonies, asking them to return to us again and again.

Indeed, we wanted even more, for individual species had powers we did not have. Plants could not only nourish us, but they could heal and comfort us. Various animals had strengths—speed, cunning, knowledge, strength, and special qualities, such as female bears leaving their winter hibernation with new life—that would greatly enhance our own lives. We begged them to assist us with their powers.

We came to understand that everything has its numinous aspect, that to encounter an animal or plant was to simultaneously encounter an animal existing in the temporal world and a numinous being that was both an individual and the totality of its species. We learned to make ourselves pitiable so that, out of compassion, these numinous beings would sometimes come to us when asked and help us, that a special relationship could be created between individual humans and particular numinous animals and plants.

Just as we understood the cosmic powers to be our parents and grandparents, so we learned that the animals and plants could be our sisters and brothers, although, out of respect and given their power, we call them by the most honorific terms we have, the ones we used for our respected elders: Grandmother and Grandfather. From our experiences, we also learned that not only is everything related, but everything is alive. Stones, moving waters, still waters, special locales, all to varying degrees had powers, powers which we could use if we but knew how. And who could better teach us than the very entities themselves? We humans learned how to communicate with the nonhuman.

Moreover, we early learned to identify ourselves in terms of these relationships. We found that considering ourselves members of extended clans, usually matrilineal, gave us protection and support when we traveled away from our own band and that this concept allowed for a degree of limited specializations. We defined these clans by attaching animal or plant names to them and so in turn created a collective linkage with the numinous aspect of these beings and a potential sharing of their powers.

In the Algonkian languages, the clans, as well as their symbolic and spiritual identification, are termed *dodem* (or dialectical variations). From the European recognition of the term in the early seventeenth century to the present, this has created confusion in the anthropological and psychological literature: the clan identification was muddled with the personal guardian spirit, gained not by birth but from visionary experiences. But this is not the place to review the considerable nonsense deriving from this confusion. To avoid adding to this confusion, all references in the following will be to personal rather than clan relationships.

Natural Plants

Modern anthropology has well demonstrated that foraging cultures are far more dependant on plants for subsistence than animals, particularly large mammals. The single exception would be the Arctic cultures that, due to the extremely limited plant resources, live primarily on caribou, seals, walrus, and whales, as well as fish. The plants are understood as directly related to Earth; they arise from Her and are dependant on Her. Removed from Her, they die. This understanding can be symbolized in a number of ways. For example, the Native peoples of

much of northern North America burn sweetgrass for its spiritually purifying smoke and otherwise use it to make baskets and
so on for the pleasant aroma it exudes. It is often braided in the
fashion that hair is worn and thus considered to be the hair of
Earth Herself.

The food supplied by wild plants, in some areas, can be sufficient to support urban populations, as a variety of grasses with
their seeds did for the early Mississippian towns. From plants
we receive not only carbohydrates but essential nutrients we
now know as vitamins and minerals. So for tens of thousands of
years we humans lived on undomesticated grains, tubers, fruits,
berries, and leaves. These plant beings not only had power over
our lives but their own intrinsic powers as well. We learned that
particular plants can heal, can increase our comfort and can
assist in our relating to other spirits.

Plants, in foraging and horticultural societies, are also
essential for the structures in which we are sheltered from the
cold and rain, supplying the framework and often the coverings
from reeds, leaves, or bark. We make mats from grasses and
shredded bark to sleep and sit upon; sometimes we weave
them into capes and blankets. We make containers from plants
for storing food and cook that food over burning wood (save on
such places as the prairies, where lack of trees led to the use of
dried bison dung).

Plant beings assist us in our rituals, not only from their
inherent sacrality, but because some can transport us into sacred
realms or allow us to perceive the sacred more clearly. Tobacco is
a powerful deity that is favored by the other spirits; in the
Americas, it is the most common gift to the spirits. Although
domesticated, until the coming of Europeans, it remained a self-
seeding, essentially wild plant. Peyote is a deity that, when used
in a proper ritual manner, enhances our abilities to communicate
with the spirit realm. Other plants, such as *datura*, may be so
potent in these regards that only certain humans with particular
abilities can utilize them without harm to themselves.

Wherever we walk, we are in the midst of plants; even in
semideserts, there is an abundance of plant beings, for we do
not live for any length of time where there are no plants at all. In
the water, we gather wild rice or the bulbs of lilies as important

food sources. Hence, not only do we live between the Earth Mother and Sky Father, but we are constantly in the midst of plant beings, all of whom have powers beyond us, and having power and being numinous are one and the same thing.

What we receive from the plant beings are the gifts of their lives so that we may live. When we gather them, we ask that they give themselves to us, and we make an offering in turn for their own. We do well never to forget that all about us are the voluntary self-sacrifices of many numinous beings. Such understanding fills us with awe and gratitude.

The gifts of plant beings are often multiple. Cedar, for example, is an especially sacred being whose leaves have healing powers; an infusion made from them can cure many illnesses. (In contemporary language, cedar leaves contain vitamin C and other important substances.) Washing in cedar water is cleansing both physically and spiritually. The smoke from the burning leaves is also spiritually purifying. We sit on cedar branches during sacred ceremonies and sleep on them at night. The bark can be shredded and woven into capes and other coverings. The wood splits readily, and the splints can be woven into baskets. Insects avoid cedar, and structures built from it are less likely to rot in damp climates. Hollowed out, large logs make light dugout canoes. Potent oils can be extracted from the wood and roots for specific medicinal uses. This list could be considerably extended. If we understand Cedar to be a living being, given all of its powers, how could we not understand it as a deity whose help we weak humans desperately need?

But the worship of undomesticated plants is hardly limited to foraging cultures. Even northern European and North American Christianity utilizes the evergreen tree from Teutonic influence in its unofficial rituals, that is, the Christmas tree. The oak was sacred in pre-Christian Britain and continued into the Christian period as the Yule log. In China, it is not unusual to come across a temple by an aged tree with a huge trunk around which is tied a red cloth, or one might find by the roots of an ancient tree a simple container for incense. As elsewhere, old trees are sacred in China in and of themselves. In the United States and Canada, so-called tree huggers continually fight to save the few remaining aged trees. Perhaps there is an unconscious Christian tendency to rid our planet of any sacred essence it cannot claim as its own.

Animals in the Wild

Humans living outside of wilderness tend to have a fear of undomesticated animals, a fear arising from the unknown. Those living in wilderness are used to being in the proximity of many animals; this proximity brings pleasure rather than apprehension. Some of my most memorable experiences include eating breakfast by the shore of a creek with a cow moose browsing her breakfast but a few feet away, quietly approaching within touching distance a deer with fawn at dawn, a fox raising her young in a den in front of my cabin porch and our mutual curiosity about each other's lives, greeting bears or bears greeting me wherever I travel or live (when in wilderness), a family of minks rushing by in a flash while I was picnicking with my family on a lakeshore, at dawn coming across a full-grown otter and a dog playing with each other on a dirt road by a stream.

Being omnivorous, we eat not only plants but animals, birds, fish, and so on. Being unfurred, we wear the skins of other beings and use their fur for blankets. Their tendons, bones, horns, all the parts of their bodies are extremely useful to us. All of these beings have powers we do not have; they are either faster, stronger, more ferocious, or even trickier—grizzly bears have been known to ambush and kill well-armed, modern hunters stalking them. Animals do not need tools, clothing, or shelter to live. Given modern weapons, hunters from urban areas still find it most difficult to kill even the small white-tailed deer. Attitude may be more important than tools.

In foraging economies, those who hunt understand not only that they are weaker than the beings they hunt, but that those beings are numinous. Rather than pit their puniness against spiritually powerful beings, they ask these beings to take pity on them. They may have their children ritually fast when they hunt so that their needs are more apparent. They ask these beings to allow themselves to be killed because humans are dependant on their gift. When the being gives itself, it is treated with gratitude

and respect. It may be given a drink of water; it may be deco-
rated; there may be ritual ways of using the animal that will be
followed as the beings have taught them. This respect does not
end with the killing, but continues through the butchering, the
cooking, the eating, and the wearing of hides. Every animal successfully hunted in this context is essentially a self-sacrifice; the
animal has given its life so that we may live. It is an understanding that should not be unfamiliar to Christians, although they
have but a single, mythohistorical instance rather than a continual one.

The giving of their lives relates to the physical aspect of
these beings; in their spiritual aspect, which continues uninter-
rupted after physical death, they are also necessary for our lives.
For in these traditions, it is understood that we are so weak we
cannot live without the protection of the spirits or deities.
Hence, infants will be given names discovered in dreams by
those who are acknowledged to have powerful relations with
the spirits in order that the children may have spiritual protec-
tors until they are old enough to seek visions and consequent
relations on their own. Most commonly, in these societies, these
relations will be with animal spirits. Cosmic spirits tend to be
more powerful and come to those who are spiritually ready to
handle such relationships.

There is no predicting which of these spirits will come to
one, although an elder guiding a youth may decide that the
spirit that came is not suitable for the individual and have the
youth try again. Given that we are dealing with polytheism, it is
not necessarily the case that a person will have a relationship
with a single spirit. Those actively involved in spiritual practices
may have a number of relationships, involving those with a
variety of talents that can be called upon as required. Nor is the
nature of the relationship with a particular animal deity the
same from person to person.

Again to give a single example, different species of Bear are
known for different powers. A relationship with the ferocious
grizzly greatly enhances a warrior's power. The more gentle
black bear, who can still kill with one swipe of her paw, is particularly known for healing power. Still one may have a relationship with the male essence of the deity, which is more warrior

oriented, than the female essence, which is more oriented toward healing in manifold ways.

Because Bear hibernates in dens, She is seen to be particularly linked with Earth. The female comes out of Earth in the spring with new life, her cubs. So She is understood to encapsulate the life-giving energies of Earth. Bears are readily observed eating various herbs when ill, healing herbs that will assist humans as well. Hence, Bear—the black bear—is considered by many traditions the most potent of the healing animal deities. Of course, She is also important to humans for Her meat, hides, and, especially, Her fat. For in the northern woods, herbivores have little fat. In this vast area, rendered bear fat is the only source of this necessary dietary supplement, as well as the basis for body paints, and is a healing unguent in its own right.

Due to the influence of turn-of-the-century Russian ethnologists and their study of reindeer-herding Siberian peoples on anthropologists and comparative religionists, as well as ethnocentrism, there is considerable misunderstanding of animal spirits in the literature. As will be discussed below in the section on domesticated animals, our relationship with them and their spiritual aspects is very different from that with nondomesticated animals. The primary error is the assumption that there is a single "Master" of each animal species and that Master is the deity, not the animals themselves. Given that we are discussing egalitarian cultures where leadership is temporary for specific tasks and accepting the leader's suggestions is voluntary and consensual, it is most unlikely that these cultures had any conception of a "master" whatsoever. Second, as we shall see for reindeer-herding cultures, where there is a spiritual head of the species, it is a she, not a he. In cultures that are in between these egalitarian cultures and highly stratified ones, such as the northern Mongolian cultures, however, there may well be an understanding of a leader of the animals, reflecting the culture's social structure, and as the cultures are patriarchal, that leader may well be a he.

The monotheistic bias tends to assume singularity, that there is a singleness to a deity. But the multiplicity inherent in polytheistic traditions is limitless. Hence, every animal we meet is both physical and spiritual. There is no actual separation between these aspects. Particularly if the animal is a powerful spirit, and especially if it is a spirit with whom we have a personal relationship, we address it as a Grandmother or Grandfather whenever we meet any member of the species, no matter if our meeting is not primarily a spiritual one. If we think of an animal species as a clan, then it will have a *dodem*, but it is the individual spirit with which we as individuals have a relationship, not its *dodem*. In other words, in foraging traditions, every being we encounter has its spiritual aspect, and we should treat it accordingly.

When such a deity comes to us in a vision, she or he teaches us what we need to know to develop the relationship. We may be taught a song and/or a ritual, be given a name, learn when and under what circumstances the deity will assist us and what our obligations are in turn. This is why it was so dangerous for me, in the story I related in the previous chapter, to naively develop a relationship before having been taught by Native elders how to do so and the implications of doing so.

Again, these obligations are confused in the literature, for everyone who develops such a relationship is given a potentially unique mode of interaction. For example, in the case of a relationship I have, I can kill the animal for others to eat and otherwise use, but I cannot eat it myself. Someone else, having a relationship with the same deity, may have the opposite mode of interaction. Or it may be only part of the animal that cannot be eaten. Or eating may be irrelevant. It is ludicrous, as one finds in the literature, to apply the same obligations to a clan *dodem*. Imagine the situation if no one in the Deer clan, in an area where venison is the major source of animal protein, could eat Deer! In any case, most animal or plant deities and clan *dodems* are not animals or plants eaten by humans. Totemism, as so many late-nineteenth-century "isms", should have long since passed away as meaningless Western imaginings of "primitive" cultures.

Animal deities are hardly limited to foraging traditions. In Manchurian culture, I have observed that anthropomorphized images of fox deities are ubiquitous in homes (although they were hidden during the Cultural Revolution). In Western traditions, Owl, the female avian spirit of the night, known in virtually all cultures, persists in living cultural memory in spite of Christianity.

Rocks and Minerals

Chinese religioaesthetics focused on Earth in its visual manifestation of "mountains and waters" (*shanshui*); these two numinous aspects of Earth were understood to be encapsulated in
water-formed rocks and stones. The focus of gardens remains
large rocks with water-driven holes through them, especially
rocks from Taihu (Great Lake) in central China. Miniature land-
scapes, in trays placed on tables, have smaller such rocks. A
favored aesthetic focus of a room would be a strange, unusual
stone, one that embodied the essence of the swirling, ever-
changing changelessness of existence in and of itself. Commonly
found in the homes of the educated would be shallow bowls
with interesting stones lying under water, to enable them to be
seen in their full brilliance as originally found. The most
renowned Chinese aesthete of all time, Mi Fu of the eleventh
century, is remembered for having deeply bowed before a particularly potent rock.

In Native American traditions, personal containers of sacred
items, whether worn around the neck or kept in sacred bundles,
commonly have stones that have captured attention as being
especially powerful or for having given themselves for this purpose. Particular sorts of stones may represent other deities, such
as Thunder, or be numinous in and of themselves. They will frequently be seen on the altars of those cultures which utilize
them, functioning as sources of power for shamanistic healing,
and so forth.

Quartz crystals, of course, are used in many cultures as a
focus or source of divine power, although the present hype of
contemporary New Age culture may be a bit overblown. For,
as with stones, it is not every crystal being that is especially
powerful or willing to assist humans. The New Age tendency
is to understand the crystal as a tool rather than a numinous
entity in and of itself as would usually be the case in polytheistic traditions:

Various minerals have been associated with human rituals
perhaps preceding homo sapiens. Neanderthals, for example,
used red ocher (powdered iron oxide) in rituals, and it, as well
as many other minerals, remain today in many traditions as

powerful sacred substances. In Native traditions, red ocher mixed with bear grease forms a sacred paint with many powerful uses.

Metals require transformation, either by beating, in the case of copper nuggets, or through sacred fire in smelting. From seemingly ordinary soil (ore) comes a substance—copper, gold, silver, and, later, bronze alloys—that glows with the light of Sun and Moon. In Indo-European mythology, the smith is a numinous figure with sacred powers. Before industrialization, metals retained a sacred aura even in Christian cultures. We need but think of the treatment of swords by warriors in Medieval European times or remember that the Grail is conceived of as formed of metal.

In Japan today, swords are still forged in lengthy, elaborate rituals by Shinto priests. When I studied the way of the sword (*kendo*) in Kyoto four decades ago, I was also trained in *iaido*, the art of drawing and killing with a single motion using an actual sword, rather than the bamboo substitute used in *kendo*.. I was taught to lay my sword before me and bow fully to it, touching my forehead to the ground, both before and after practice. The sword is treated with the greatest reverence because it has a *kami* nature; that is, it is itself sacred.

In China, for the first two millennia of its civilization, cast bronze ritual vessels were its most sacred paraphernalia, buried with rulers and a repository for the sacred oaths cast onto the surface of their interior. In the Great Lakes region of North America, as far back as several thousand years ago, copper was understood to be the bones of an extremely powerful and dangerous underwater deity. It was made into beautiful objects and treated with great respect. It is still the preferred material for ritual items in that area. In Mesoamerica and the Andes, gold and silver, the sweat of Sun and tears of Moon, were sacred substances, deities in and of themselves, to be used in religious rituals and to represent other deities. The European ruthless, passionate desire for and hoarding of these beings for nonsacred purposes was never understood.

In modern Western culture, we surround ourselves with all of these beings but with no sense of their own intrinsic existence, let alone their potential power and meanings.

Monotheism tends to desacralize our environments, and we are the poorer for it.

Domesticated Plants

Our reliance on plants eventually led to their domestication, and this leads to a different understanding of plants from that of nondomesticated ones. These plants do not give themselves; we must nurture them ourselves. Rather than being divine in and of themselves, they tend to be understood as the gift of Earth or of the Garden, as a related but separate deity.

In China, farmers do not make offerings to the domesticated plants but to the images of Grandmother and Grandfather Soil in a shrine, usually by the farmed field or at a nearby sacred site, as well as to their images at the central spot on the household altar, the ancestral tablets off to the side. The crops are Earth's gift, and Hers to withhold if we are not properly respectful.

Native North American cultures offer the sacred Tobacco to Earth directly on the fields at planting time. The primary domesticants—corn, beans, and squash—are known by Iroquoian-speaking peoples as the Three Sisters, daughters of Earth. Corn is understood to grow from the breasts of the recumbent Earth. Given that the juice of fresh corn kernels has a milky appearance, this is a most natural understanding. In Amazonia, the women sing to Earth, begging Her for food, as the men do with regard to hunting, and make offerings of sacred substances. The tallest plant may be understood as the mother of all the other similar plants and must be treated with the greatest of respect or She may shit weeds.

In Hellenistic culture, at the heart of the Eleusynian esoteric initiations was the vision by the initiands of Earth and Her daughter, Grain, attained by eating a sacred bread or drinking an infusion of sacred grain, possibly infected with the psychoactive ergot of rye. (The initiation was esoteric and so moving to the hundreds of thousands of initiands over time that the details have never been revealed.) This understanding, ubiquitous in all horticultural and agricultural traditions save the monotheistic ones, even survived in Christian Europe. For example, the ubiquitous Black Madonnas often seem to function as grain deities, replacing the indigenous ones present before the domination of Christianity. Western farmers may be Christian but, save for the utterly mechanized agribusiness megafields, tend to still reverence the soil and its gifts as having a sacred aura, although this will be unstated. We only have to watch the face of a small-scale farmer run soil through his hands or patiently and raptly stare at the growing plants to recognize this human response to Her and Her gifts.

Domesticated Animals

As essential plants on which we subsist came to be domesticated, so too did the animals on which we depended. The most recent shift of this type is to be found with the Eurasian sub-Arctic peoples, who domesticated the reindeer a few centuries ago, perhaps stimulated by the cattle and sheep herds of peoples who lived south of them. As with plants, this transition changes the religious understanding of the animals, as well as the affiliated rituals. Rather than it being understood, as in foraging traditions, that the animals as numinous beings sacrificed themselves for the welfare of humans, now humans sacrifice selected domesticated animals, whose raising is the responsibility of humans, to the numinous being understood to be ultimately responsible for the gift of these animals.

The sacrifice of domesticated animals is ubiquitous to human cultures save for the monotheistic ones. And in two of the Religions of the Book, Islam and Judaism, animals are still ritually slaughtered by a religious specialist, who is, to all intents and purposes, a priest. Indeed, sacrifice of these animals is so pervasive, that, until modern times, in most cultures, only sacrificed domesticated animals were eaten by humans living in these cultures.

Because formal, ritualized sacrifice as sacrifice ceased in the precursor to the monotheistic traditions with the destruction of the Israelite temple in 70 CE, sacrifice has also ceased to be understood in these traditions. This is especially the case with Christianity, because it used the metaphor of sacrifice for the execution of Jesus, the "Lamb of God." What has been lost is the understanding that sacrificed animals are not wasted. Sacrifice means that the meat is first offered to the deities or other spirits before humans eat it. This is as true for human sacrifice as any other, and this intention is partially kept by those Christian traditions that have a doctrine of transubstantiation; that is, the bread and wine of the Eucharist actually becomes the flesh and blood of Christ when ingested. This is why the centralization of sacrificial altars in the temple at Jerusalem caused such political turmoil. It meant that anytime people wanted to eat meat, they had to take the animal to Jerusalem to be sacrificed. From a polytheistic perspective, another drawback to monotheism is its centralizing tendency.

In the early periods of domestication, the animals are virtually part of human families. It is probably no accident that there is a linkage in the Jewish foundation myth of the Patriarchs of a ram and a son. The ram could be substituted for Isaac because the ram would have been seen as a close approximation.

As hunted animals were the source of rich animal protein and fats in foraging cultures, so the domestic animals have the same role in herding or horticultural and agricultural societies. And just as we do not require rich foods on a daily basis but do need them periodically for health and growth, so too domestic animals were not eaten on a daily basis until the rise of stratified societies marked by the daily eating of meat by the elite, a practice requiring the inefficient feeding of rich grains to animals rather than humans. Mengzi, twenty-four hundred years ago in China, succinctly criticized the practice, when ordinary people were starving, as "feeding humans to the animals."

Hence, the sacrifice of animals was associated with ritual feasts, which supplied both nutritional and spiritual needs. In traditional Chinese culture, among the nonelite, the meat of mammals—cattle, pigs, and goats or sheep—is eaten at sacrificial feasts on average twice a month, when resources were available. At the time of the Israelite temple, meat would have been eaten less frequently by most, since people were required to make offerings at the temple but a few times a year (while special bread was offered to Asherah or the Queen of Heaven far more frequently).

Among the Saami on the Kola Peninsula in present-day Russia, reindeer are sacrificed to *Pots-Hosjik* and *Luot-Hosjik*, *pots* referring to the domesticated reindeer and *luot* referring to the wild, hunted reindeer. *Hosjik* is Russian, not Saami, for "mistress." It seems that reindeer herding developed along with a sense of hierarchical social structure which came from the stratified societies to the south, for the original term for undomesticated reindeer was *mintis*, with no reference to a superior of the reindeer. This lexical development supports the understanding that the hunted animals are individually numinous, while the domesticated animals of the same species are not perceived as numinous in and of themselves but are the gift of a divinity, in this case, the Mistress of the Reindeer Herds.

There is another kind of being often discussed as domesticated that is treated quite differently: dogs (this is also true of cats, but as I am a "dog person" and have limited experience with cats, I had best keep silent with regard to them). There is a further potential nuance in this regard: that we did not domesticate dogs but that they domesticated us. In any case, dogs early formed hunting partnerships with humans to their mutual advantage. For dog lovers, dogs are not animals; they are family. And dogs appear to feel the same way about us. But dogs are sacrificed and eaten. In China, dog meat is considered very special and there are still a number of injunctions with regard to eating it. In Native American and at least some Central African traditions, the sacrifice of a dog is essential to certain major ritual feasts. One Nakota (Siouan language culture), initially raised fully in the Native tradition in the late nineteenth century before receiving a Western education, writes of being required, on leaving childhood, to sacrifice that which was most precious to him. Anyone who had a dog companion as a child will understand what it meant to that boy to sacrifice his dog. What is being suggested here is that dog sacrifices are a substitute for human sacrifices; we perceive dogs as closer to us than to animals per se.

Similarly, there is a circumpolar bear sacrifice still practiced by traditionalist Ainu. An infant bear is captured and raised as a human child, even suckled at the breast. When full grown, the bear is sacrificed. I would theorize, having no experience with the culture, that domestication of this bear transforms it from a divinity, as undomesticated animals are, especially Bear, to a quasi human. This bear then is a stand-in for the sacrifice of a human, as is the dog. In summary, domestication transforms animals, as well as plants, from deities in and of themselves to beings that can be offered to deities—we share this offering after the spiritual essence is consumed, by feasting on the meat.

Modes of Interaction

If the deities did not communicate with us, we would not know about them. Even Western theologies, much as they proceed using the tools of formal logic, ultimately derive from revelation, made manifest in the Bible or through the Qu'ran. Save for the charismatic aspects of the Religions of the Book, for most adherents, the revelations accordingly are indirect. But in the traditions which are economically dependant on undomesticated plants and animals, the relationship with divinity is different; virtually every individual will communicate directly with divinity and receive revelations in response.

This mode of interaction is termed "shamanism" in modern Western culture, a term that has engendered much confusion and misunderstanding. The term is a westernization, via the addition of "ism," of a term found in Altaic Tungistic languages: Śaman. In Tungistic-speaking and other contiguous cultures, which have long ceased to be foraging cultures and are, to varying degrees, hierarchical, shamans are persons who interact with the spirit realm for their family or community. This shaman may inherit the position or have a particular talent in this regard. Most of the early studies of shamanism were written by Russian scholars familiar with the Orthodox Church and the concept of priests who alone can perform the major sacred functions due to the sacrament of ordination. What is generally not understood in this literature is that all members of shamanistic communities have the same abilities and understandings as the shaman but not to the same degree, due to the greater training and practice of the specialist or stronger relevant innate endowments, that is, talent. In other cultures, such as the egalitarian ones of Native America, all individuals traditionally functioned as shamans to varying degrees, hence, the term "democratized shamanism" found in the American anthropological literature since the 1930s.

The term "shamanism" is further confused in the English and, more recently, central European anthropological literature due to the inclusion of spirit possession under the rubric of shamanism, thus bringing in the cultures of Africa, South and East Asia, and Oceania. In other words, "shamanism" is now being applied to virtually all of the traditions of the world save for the Religions of the Book, and the "ism" aspect leads to an understanding that somehow this supposed all-encompassing "religion" has considerable coherence. Finally, New Age religion, with its modern focus on the individual, proffers a shamanism divorced from community. One can pay a substantial fee, spend time at a weekend workshop, and become a "shaman," here meaning learning how to have a spiritual experience, training which any Pentecostal Church will offer gratis, voluntary contributions accepted.

Furthermore, in all traditions labelled as shamanic, there is not a single term for those who engage with spirits in healing, divining, and so on, but a range of terms describing different specialties and means of working. For example, in the Anishnabe tradition mentioned above, there are four terms for such persons in general. A similar situation exists among Siberian peoples. The peoples in these cultures take shamanic functioning for granted; it is a continuum in which all, to varying degrees, take part. More important to them are the deities themselves. Focussing on a particular human individual, rather than the deities, seems to be a modern Western predilection, probably arising from the modern West's focus on individualism and the Roman Catholic and Orthodox Christian reliance on priests.

In foraging traditions or those maintaining the religious aspects of such cultures in the contemporary period, people are taught to seek relationships with divinities from an early age. In the psychotropic-plant-using cultures of the Amazonian basin, vision-inducing substances are given to infants (as well as dogs), so that they can begin to perceive "reality." In the cultures of northern North America which focus on fasting for visions, children are encouraged to fast at a young age, although but for brief periods of time when very young. In the American southwest, running long distances is the technique utilized to stimulate visions, and again children are encouraged to do this. Hence, by adolescence, individuals will have already forged relationships with particular deities through trance experiences. These relationships will be most influential on chosen lifestyles, given that all accomplishments are understood to require the aid of spirits. The deity with whom one is connected will have much to do with the work in which one may specialize, according to the specialization that the deity is understood to have.

Visions may come even when not actively sought. Lucid dreams, here understood as dreams which are remembered because of their importance to one's life, are generally not distinguished from deliberately induced visions. (In psychology, "lucid dreaming" specifically refers to the type of dreams in which one is aware that one is dreaming.) In many languages, the same term is used for lucid dreams and visions. Encounters need not be visionary. Since the animals, plants, stones, and so forth that one encounters have their spiritual aspect, one learns to respectfully greet and speak to these beings, and they may communicate in return. As related in chapter 1, this happened to me even before I learned to do this or expected this kind of communication. Of course, being untrained, at that time I but poorly understood the experiences.

People will often seek the advice of elders to understand their experiences better, as the communications are not always clear. One also must learn patience; perhaps, as a Westerner, for me this was the hardest lesson of all. I did not receive explicit understanding of my relationships with the two deities most important to me until twenty-four years after the initial revelations or contacts. In the autobiographies of visionaries throughout the world we will often find that visions received in adolescence were not fully understood until much later in life. Another deity made contact with me years ago but has not yet imparted the nature or purpose of the relationship, but I have learned to be patient. Deities can also come to one indirectly. Many years ago, a deity attempted to make a connection with my wife as I was becoming involved with these relationships, but she was disinclined to enter into such an association. Subsequently, I asked the deity if She would assist me instead when necessary and She did.

While visions are often individualistic, they may also be communal. In cultures utilizing psychoactive substances, a skilled leader can enable a group to have a common vision. Similarly, the "spirit lodge" rituals described in chapter 2 can, but do not necessarily, lead to the sharing of an individual's vision. Such communal visions enhance group activities, particularly difficult or dangerous ones. Hence, rituals for sharing experiences precede group hunts in the Amazon and, for the ritual leaders, precede major rituals in Native North America (as they once did communal hunts and group raids).

Ceremonies with a number of participants in which all have their own connections with individual deities are different from those in traditions in which the participants are dependant on ritual leaders for these connections. We do not need to leave the monotheistic traditions to find these differences. In both Judaism and Islam, individuals are periodically required to pray communally, but within the communion they individually pray directly to God. The ritual leader is not an intermediary but merely sets the pace. Anyone familiar with the rituals can lead them. In contrast, in Catholic, Orthodox, and similar Christian traditions, adherents must receive sacraments from an ordained priest who mediates the relationship between worshiper and deity. This difference is even stronger in the polytheistic traditions being discussed. For anyone's deity may enter the rituals, aside from those that may be the focus of the rituals.

I have attended major ceremonies, usually of four day's duration, where it was announced that a new ritual would be added that day following an individual's dream, and we were instructed on how to prepare for it. At other ceremonies, such as a Thirst Dance (known in the literature as the "Sun Dance"), seemingly passive observers were actually calling on their connections with divinities to assist individual dancers (those offering self-sacrifice) or the ceremony as a whole. No mention is made of this, even if there are major effects such as a thunderstorm changing direction and skirting the ceremonial grounds. We have to know the individuals, their connections, and resultant abilities to have a sense of what is going on about us.

Every activity in these traditions is understood to require the assistance of the deities. Women receive dreams for the designs they put on clothing, and these designs bring some of the power of the deity to the wearer. One dreams where and when to hunt, where and what to gather for food. Healers must dream what medicines are needed for a specific person's illness, where to find it, and how to gather and use it. One dreams what activities to engage in and how to carry them out. All of these dreams come from specific deities.

Here again the literature grossly tends to misrepresent shamanism. Often the shaman is described as one who can control the spirits. This is absurd. The spirits are far more powerful than any human. What the shaman strives for is to encourage the spirit to assist humans, even though, as in Inuit traditions, this may involve wrestling with the spirit. The purpose is not to conquer, which is impossible, but to placate it. (The biblical story of Jacob wrestling with an angel may be a reflection of this practice.)

In all of these instances, the action is never for oneself. This is a commonality throughout so-called shamanistic cultures. Modern Western individualism is not the primary mode of existence in other cultures. To carry out activities for oneself, especially to do so with the aid of spirits, is the only evil perceived in the cultures being discussed. In the cultures that I am familiar with, it is understood that any such evil falls back on the individual and their family, ultimately leading to death. In some other traditions of which I am aware, those understood so to act are considered an extremely dangerous threat to the community and are likely to be killed. These are egalitarian societies in which prestige comes from giving possessions away rather than accumulating them. Hence, anyone perceived as being far better off than others in the community is liable to be suspected of evil sorcery, sometimes called, in these communities, "witchcraft."

Negative power is also conventionally used against traditional enemies, but, as this is done in support of one's own community, it is considered positive behavior. Accidents and illnesses tend to be viewed as the effects of the application of such power, and one known to have powerful relationships with the numinous may be asked to deal with the problem. Such a person, using his or her own power, must then find who is perpetrating the accidents or illness and then counter the wielder of that negative power. This is a dangerous task, as the wielder of the power, if good at it, will know who is countering her or him and counterattack. The person with the most powerful connections or the more powerful deities will, in effect, win and survive. Other illness may be perceived as due to the influence of negative spirits; healing requires exorcising these negative powers with the aid of one's spirit connections.

It is these actions, particularly the ability to affect persons and things at a distance, that conflicts with Western reasoning. Western theorists have been comfortable with shamanic healing by equating it with faith healing, both dismissed as temporary effects based on the belief of the patient in the efficacy of the healer (an important constituent of Western medicine as well, as many modern studies have demonstrated); in other words, the healing is assumed to affect only psychosomatic illnesses. This supposed explanation collapses with healing or other effects at a distance, especially if the person affected is unaware of these actions.

Having a Western scientific education, which I still utilize, and imbued with Buddhist nontheism, I was hardly prone to accept readily the simplest explanation: that it is the deities who, in cooperation with the healer, effect these events. Having visions and other interactions with deities can be meaningful yet understood as the workings of the subconscious and so on. Work at a distance voids these types of explanations. I have Native friends, one of whom spiritually travels to observe the patient, who heal at a distance, although it is not the preferred way. I myself, fused with a deity, have made observations at places I have never physically been, and these observations were confirmed in detail by those who did know the place. I have gone to people in a similar fashion, when absolutely necessary for a community, who did not know me and whose immediate subsequent behavior would be otherwise inexplicable. Parapsychological terminology is less than useful in these regards, as they are but terms that have no intrinsic explanations. Following the logical maxim of accepting the simplest explanation led me to realize that I was indeed a polytheist, to my surprise, and, eventually, resulted in this treatise.

CHAPTER FOUR

THE FAMILY DEIFIED: ANCESTRAL SPIRITS

❖

[T]he timelessness of all time. This is eternity. This is Pō.... In Pō there dwell our ancestors, transfigured into gods. They are forever god-spirits, possessing the strange and awesome power of the gods. Yet they are forever our relatives, having for us the loving concern a mother feels for her infant, or a grandfather for his first-born grandson. As gods and relatives in one, they give us strength when we are weak, warning when danger threatens, guidance in our bewilderment, inspiration in our arts. They are equally our judges, hearing our words and watching our actions, reprimanding us for error, and punishing us for blatant offense. For these are our godly ancestors. These are our spiritual parents. These are our aumākua. *... We in our time shall become* aumākua *to our descendants even yet unborn.*

—Mary Kawena Pukui (Hawaiian), *Nānā I Ke Kumu (Look to the Source)*

Ancestral Spirits

Foraging cultures are usually seminomadic, ranging over a defined territory as the seasons make available different foods.

59

The dead may be buried, deposited in caves, or placed on platforms at locations which tend to otherwise be avoided. The dead are honored but also kept at a distance. Some cultures, after a final memorial ceremony at the end of the mourning period, ask the dead not to return; others may avoid mentioning the names of the dead.

Horticulture brings a habitation change. Fields are brought under cultivation and gardened for ten- to fifteen-year periods. When the soil becomes infertile, the people move a short distance and create new gardens or move to old ones that have regenerated in the intervening time. The gardens support a larger population, and people often live in large dwellings or longhouses, in matrilineal and matrilocal clan groupings. The dead are buried nearby, sometimes under the floor of the dwelling, even under bed platforms, as at Çatalhöyük in central Anatolia, the earliest known permanent, substantial town based on horticulture or agriculture, dating to nearly nine thousand years ago. Or the dead may be burned, reduced to ashes which are added to liquid and consumed by the clan members. Rather than being avoided, the dead are always present. When periodic moves took place, the dead were often brought along, either as skulls, as among some Amazonian cultures, or bundles of bones, as among the Iroquoian speaking people around Lake Ontario at the time of contact with Europeans.

The clan dwellings allow for multigenerational habitation, the ability to care for the aged, and a sense of caring for the respected elders after death. Their advice is still needed, still sought. Sleeping above their bones may engender dreams by which the dead can communicate with the living. It was found that the dead elders, ever present in the mind, could continue to communicate with their family by speaking through the mouth of an entranced living member of the family. This is how I assume spirit possession began, for it is found in virtually all living horticultural and early-type agricultural societies around the planet, save for the Americas. Even there, although spirit possession seems not to have been practiced, dead leaders were revered in the agricultural traditions. For example, in the Andean civilizations, the dead were mummified, the rulers, male and female, placed in temples where they were fed and cared for by their living descendants. Undoubtedly, they had means for communicating with them.

Ancestral spirits are not deities, but they are understood as more than human. They often are perceived to exist in a realm between human and divine, and they can mediate between the two. They have powers beyond the living, and those powers can be used to the advantage of the living. The living feed and otherwise care for the family dead; the dead seek to enhance the fortunes of their family. Family comes to be recognized as extending through time in both directions. From the past, the dead continue to relate to the family, so long as the living keep them well. Both seek to continue the family, so as to continue their own existence in the spirit realm; the future is as crucial to the family as is the past.

Throughout sub-Saharan Africa, South Asia, East Asia, and Oceania, the deities directly interact with humans through spirit possession, and, in all of these many traditions, the dead of the family are greatly revered. In the past, this was also true of the eastern Mediterranean and Mesopotamian civilizations, including early Israelite culture. The next chapter will concern itself with non family dead as deities; the subject of this chapter is the family dead.

China

In a traditional Chinese home, whether it be a single-room dwelling or the Imperial Palace ("Forbidden City") covering an enormous area with many buildings, the focus will be an altar. In a single-room dwelling, the altar will be centered against the wall facing the entrance; in the palace, it will be in a temple building at the center of the massive compound. The purpose of the altar will be to enshrine the family dead, indicated by name tablets. In the homes of ordinary people, over time, the altar has become complex, also enshrining the deities discussed in chapter 2 and in the next chapter, but the understanding that its raison d'être is the family dead remains.

In a simple traditional home of one or several rooms, the arrangement of furniture is relatively standard. Under the high rectangular altar is slid a square table that will be brought out at the time of sacrificial offerings. In front of this arrangement is a circular dining table; along the walls are chairs for nondining seating. The shrine room is the main room of the family; when the family members gather to eat or talk, the dead are always present.

In front of the ancestral tablets, the furnishings are again culturally standardized. Before the tablets are a container for holding incense and three small cups for wine. To the sides are set a pair of candle holders for red candles, or their electric approximations, and a pair of vases for flowers. In front of all, especially in warmer climes, is a bowl of fruit. Every morning the mistress of the home offers incense and prays to the spirits of the family dead. From Beijing to Toronto, these ritual paraphernalia are available in general and grocery stores catering to Chinese.

In contemporary style homes, particularly of the upper middle class, there is some elaboration of this schema. Since homes now tend to be multistoried, while traditional architecture spread horizontally, a recent trend has been to make the uppermost room a shrine room, it having a porch to replace the traditional front courtyard where offerings can safely be burned in a small furnace.

When a person dies, particularly an older person who has been successful in life (for a male, by enhancing the fortunes of the family, and for a female, by producing heirs), considerable care and expense is taken to ensure the spiritual comfort of the deceased. Daoist priests are hired to carry out elaborate funerals, and, after a set number of days, Buddhist monks or nuns will be hired to chant sutras. Money will be donated to temples to enshrine a small name tablet so that the prayers there will also benefit the deceased. Elaborate offerings of furnished paper homes, clothing, automobiles, televisions, VCRs, and so on will be burned for the use of the deceased in the realm of the dead. The tomb will be carefully situated, according to the advice of fengshui experts (the original and primary purpose of fengshui) to enhance the deceased's comfort and power and, thereby, their living family's fortune.

Approximately twice a month, according to the lunar calendar of ceremonies, elaborate sacrificial meals will be offered before the family shrine, the food placed on the square table mentioned above. Also offered, through burning, will be "spirit money" and paper representations of gold and silver ingots. Nowadays, these are being replaced by checkbooks and credit cards drawn on the Bank of the Realm of the Dead (translated into English as "The Bank of Hell," since Christian missionaries told the Chinese that that is the Western name for where their dead, as heathens, will end up). The family respectfully waits until the dead are satiated, determined through the use of thrown divining blocks. The food is then removed to the circular dining table where the living eat the material remains of the food. It is a family banquet in which the dead are the honored diners.

On certain of these occasions, if there is a clan temple nearby, the food will first be offered to the dead before their ancestral tablets there, prior to the offering in the family home. Once a year, the food and wine are brought to the grave for the initial offering. At another festival, an opera may be put on, or now electronically reproduced, at the graveyard for the entertainment of the dead. All festivals include an offering to the family dead, regardless of their overt purpose. All changes in the family—marriage, births, accomplishments such as graduations and promotions, and so on—are reported to the dead by announcing it before the enshrined tablets.

To make sense of this pattern, it should be understood that in all nonmonotheistic cultures, souls are understood to be multiple. How else could one, for example, soul travel? One soul journeys and one must remain with the body or it would die. Hence, in China it is understood that one soul remains with the corpse and in the realm of the dead (originally solely underground, but now simultaneously in the Western Paradise), and another soul is housed in the name tablets (and, in the distant past, was amalgamated with Sky, as the other was in Earth).

The fortunes of the family are dependant on the well-being of the dead members of the family, and the fortunes of the clan on its larger set of dead. Unless the dead are kept well, they will not have sufficient power to assist the family, and unless the dead are pleased, they may not care to help the family. Hence, if there are problems in the family with regard to their fortunes, health, or family strife, it is necessary to consult with the dead to determine the root of the problem. Specialists are engaged to do this, and the means for doing so are multiple, depending on the modus operandi of the specialist. A few will travel with the aid of spirits to seek out the dead, speak to them, and then report back. More commonly, a medium will be possessed by a deity who will then accomplish this task. Not uncommon is for a medium to be possessed by the dead who will then directly communicate with the members of the family. The family can then act to rectify the concerns of the dead, and hopefully matters will improve.

The family and clan dead are not deities, but they are numinous. Nonfamily dead can become deities, but that phenomenon will be dealt with in the next chapter. The dead of ruling clans, however, may be in an intermediary state, for the ruling clans tend to be understood to be descended from deities or semideities. The first ruling dynasty for which we have remnants of their origin myth was descended from an avian spirit. The next ruling dynasty for which we have the complete origin myth was descended from a major culture hero (culture heroes are the topic of chapter 6). My wife's natal clan is a branch of the last imperial clan, and, according to this clan's detailed written records, which we had a chance to see, she is descended from a bird-headed, human-bodied spirit.

For the first two millennia of kingship and the following imperial government, relations with the clan dead were even closer than they have been in the last thousand years, with regard to both divination and spirit possession. From perhaps three to four millennia in the past, the rulers consulted with Shangdi ("The Powers on High"), primarily through pyroscapulamancy (a circumpolar mode of divination based on heat applied to scapulae), with regard to every important, and sometimes not so important, decision. From the mid-nineteenth century, Protestant missionaries used "Shangdi" as a translation for "God," and subsequent Protestant-influenced scholars wrote that the Chinese in the past worshipped a monotheistic male God up in the sky, where He properly belongs. The mass of surviving oracular writings cannot support such a Eurocentric interpretation. Shangdi was the amalgam of the deceased of the ruling clan, and it was to make food and wine offerings to them that the rulers utilized most of the society's surplus production in the casting of elaborate bronze sacrificial vessels.

That the spiritual powers of the ancestors can be understood as a collective, as well as there being a term for such an amalgamation, is far from unusual in the many cultures which consider the family dead to be powerful spirits. For example, in Kiwai culture of the western gulf of Papua, the collective power of the ancestors is termed "imuni."

From nearly three thousand years ago in China, we have odes from the sacrificial rituals of the ruling clan that describe the procedures, procedures that accord with the later writing of ritual texts for imperial and elite clans in the early imperial period. These rituals began with the sacrificer, the son or daughter-in-law (depending on the sex of the recipient) of the primary deceased to whom the sacrifice is being offered, divining for an auspicious day for the sacrifice and the identity of the person who will be the Incorporator of the Dead, usually the grandson or granddaughter-in- law of the recipient. The Incorporator of the Dead fasts and meditates for seven days preceding the sacrifice, the last four intensely, constantly visualizing the life and appearance of the sacrifice's recipient. All those who meet him or her treat the person as if meeting the dead recipient. When the Incorporator of the Dead travels to the clan temple for the sacrifice, even the emperor, should he happen to come across him, must dismount from his chariot and bow respectfully to him, as one would to a powerful spirit. At the sacrifice, the Incorporator of the Dead drinks the wine and eats the food directed to the sacrifice's recipient. She or he drinks nine large cups of wine (after a lengthy fast). The Master of Ceremonies announces that "The Spirits are Drunk." They have arrived in the body of the Incorporator of the Dead, and they bless the recipients through her. The Incorporator of the Dead then leaves, and it is announced that the spirits have returned to their abode in the sky. All then repair to dining halls, females and males separately, to drink the wine and eat the now despiritized sacrificial food, happy with the blessings bestowed on the clan by the ancestral spirits.

Given the frequency of the sacrificial feasts and that the Incorporator of the Dead was usually in late adolescence, a period of acute spiritual interest for many, we can assume that virtually all of the youth and their spouses, if married by then, were bonded to the clan by this intense experience of being the physical host for the clan dead. It is necessary to try to understand what it would mean to a person who gives his or her body after intense, prolonged contemplation of the dead person, to allow a beloved grandfather (or grandmother-in-law) to eat a fine banquet and be again among the living members of the family. In middle age, the same youth will now host the sacrificial offering to his own father and his wife to his mother. Death is not an ending of family relationship; it is a transformation into a spirit whose relationship with the family does not change. One hopes to live to old age, for only as a clan elder, whether male or female, can one have a degree of individuality in a culture where family comes first and foremost. Death, after old age, is a continuation into a new mode of existence, where one is no longer revered by one's family but worshipped. It is when one can directly influence the numinous realm to help the fortunes of one's family.

Twentieth-century Western scholars, often from liberal Protestant backgrounds and following a long tradition, to be discussed in chapter 7, of using an imagined Chinese intelligentsia as forerunners of the European Enlightenment, understood the Chinese elite to be, at most, agnostic about the existence of deities. This understanding was reinforced by interpretations, with which Chinese scholars disagreed, of early texts. In retrospect, such interpretation indicates a profound misunderstanding of not only polytheism, but of family. It is not just we humans who do not turn from those we love after death. Elephants, whales, and chimpanzees will stay around the dead, often for days, mourning their loss. And do they die in their memories? The Chinese position is that our parents nurtured and cared for us as infants and children, and so we care for them in old age and after death. We continue to feed them, and they continue to care for us.

With an understanding of a wide range of numinous entities, outside of the monotheistic traditions, humans tend to perceive of the dead of the family as continuing to be influential on their lives, whether understood as spirits or not. Until we literally lose our memories, the dead with whom our lives were intimately connected are still with us. It does not take an act of faith, in the sense of Christian theology, to believe we have or had mothers and fathers, grandfathers and grandmothers. To conceive of individuals in this intense family cultural milieu being agnostic about their dead parents or grandparents demonstrates the height of ethnocentric arrogance and ignorance.

Offering incense daily and food periodically to our deceased parents is not done out of fear of a wrathful God but out of love for our dear ones. Seeking their advice and help is not done out of duty; it but repeats a pattern set when we were children. For those living in such a family web, there is little worry over life after death, so long as we have children of like minds. As we care for our deceased parents and grandparents, so we will be cared for by our children and grandchildren. Old people do not fear death under these circumstances, but look forward to its eventuality. If we can afford it, we purchase our coffin and grave clothes while still in good health. It is comforting to be able to admire the home and clothes for the body after death, to show them off to friends, to know with certainty that after death we will become a spirit well looked after by our children and grandchildren and have the opportunity to look after them as a numinous entity. It is a timeless continuum. If we are part of a clan with a recorded past, we then exist in an even larger network of persons and of time, and we have a greater obligation for its continuance (not necessarily an advantageous understanding, given the present extreme global overpopulation).

The Chinese rituals of ancestor reverence spread into contiguous cultures: Korea, Vietnam, Japan, and Manchuria. These were not necessarily entirely new rituals that were adopted. As can be found among the original Oceanic inhabitants of Taiwan, a ritual relationship with the dead of family and clan was ubiquitous throughout East and Southeast Asia, as well as the cultures of the Pacific Islands. Rather it seems that the systematized articulation of Chinese culture overlay patterns already present.

My wife, who as a young child left mainland China at the end of the civil war with her family for Taiwan, had been cut off from her larger family, that is, all of her relatives save the nuclear family. As political circumstances changed nearly four decades later, she and I went back with our children to meet her natal family. We were met at the train station in the early hours of the morning by a horde of people, all family. After meeting her grandfather for the first time, we were taken a distance to the family's ancestral home area to announce her return at the tomb of her grandmother, offering her favorite foods, liquor, and cigarettes. A half dozen years later, we returned with my wife's mother for the spring tomb-offering ceremony. It took a bus to bring all her children, virtually all of her grandchildren, and some great-grandchildren, along with spouses, to her tomb to make the offerings.

For me, from a different culture, this was a beautiful outpouring of love. Until Vatican II, for Christian missionaries, from the same larger culture in which I was brought up, and continuing so for Protestant missionaries, this is intolerable Devil worship. From their polytheistic perspective, the Chinese understand Protestant missionaries to be saying that love and respect for family members is to cease on death or the jealousy of the wrathful monotheistic God will be aroused. For loving and caring for their dead parents and grandparents, they will be consigned to eternal torture in hell, where their dead relatives are already suffering. At least for Catholics there are funeral masses and the ability to pray for loved ones in purgatory. And for Jews, there are memorial days with candles and special prayers; dead parents are yearly remembered by their children on the anniversary of their death. Hence, polytheistic traditions can have as much difficulty in understanding monotheistic cultures as monotheistic traditions have in understanding polytheistic ones.

Modes of Communication

If the dead are important to the living, then the living must be able to interrelate with them. The two common means worldwide are divination, an indirect form of communication, and spirit possession, a direct means. The Chinese early used pyroscapulamancy, the heating of a small part of a scapula of an animal (as well as the plastron of tortoises) leading to cracks in the bone which are then interpreted. This technique is used in several circumpolar foraging and reindeer-herding cultures, its furthest extension from northern Eurasia being the native traditions of the St. Lawrence River area in eastern Canada. In the latter case, as in the northern cultures, the communication is not with the dead of the family but with animal deities. Another common means is repeatedly casting a number of the same objects and interpreting the accumulated pattern. The Chinese primarily used milfoil stalks; central West Africans utilize shells or small bones. In both these cases, the divination may be with the dead or with deities. Of course, there are many other modes of divination as well.

What seems particular to horticultural and agricultural societies, with few exceptions, is a combination of a continuing relationship with the dead and spirit possession. Possible exceptions are Indo-European-speaking cultures, uninfluenced by other cultures, and the native traditions of the Americas, where, although the dead were important in the agricultural societies, the mode of interacting with the spirits continued the means used in foraging and herding cultures discussed in the previous chapter. Indo-European-speaking cultures seem to have originally been horse-utilizing, cattle-herding ones, and they also used the methods of communicating with the spirit realm found in the northern climes. Hence, in India the synthesis between the Indo-European Aryan culture and the indigenous Dravidian traditions, linked to the Mesopotamian ones, led to a limited number of rituals oriented toward the family dead and spirit possession within another type of sacrificial religious system. Similarly, in the Himalayan regions, with the mixing of Central and South Asian types of ecstatic religious functioning, we find religious specialists who function both shamanically and mediumistically. That is, there are specialists who combine working in trance with cooperating spirits, while maintaining awareness and will, as discussed in the preceding chapter, with being possessed by spirits who use the specialist's body as the spirits' will, of which the specialist often has no awareness or memory. Such a synthesis seems also to have taken place in Hellenic culture, as other Indo-European-speaking groups of people slowly filtered into the eastern Mediterranean area, to be discussed in the next chapter. In Roman culture, there were shrines in the home to the family dead to which offerings were made as in many other polytheistic traditions.

We could posit that spirit possession begins with the closer relationship with the dead, the dead of one's family, that develops with horticulture. The dead becoming perceived as functional spirits leads to an anthropomorphizing of the deities in place of the plant and animal deities of foraging cultures. For example, the Manchurian fox deity mentioned in the preceding chapter is perceived in human form. Spirit possession then becomes the means for interacting with anthropomorphic spirits as well, especially in agricultural societies, with the exceptions mentioned above.

One can fuse with animal spirits while functioning as a shaman; that is, one can become the spirit while maintaining one's own identity, as I have experienced, or one can bring the spirit into oneself, as, it seems, some others do, but this is not the same as allowing the spirit to displace one in one's body. Indeed, it is difficult to imagine this happening in foraging cultures. What would a human body be like if completely, not partially, an animal or plant? Would it still be able to interact with the community? The shaman must maintain an intermediary role for effective interaction to take place.

With human spirits and divinities, it is a different situation. They know how to use our bodies and how to speak to people. They need our bodies to do this directly; they do not need us in our bodies. To be taken over by an unknown spirit is a frightening experience; all societies, including Christian ones, have exorcism rituals to remove an undesirable possessing spirit. But to allow a loved one to temporarily use our body is different. This is a familiar spirit, a desirable one. We would welcome it, and this, I suspect, is the origin of functional spirit possession. That is, spirit possession may have originated in human culture through a living member of a family being temporarily possessed by a deceased family member when the family desired to communicate with that dead person.

With the development of spirit possession, the living and the dead members of the family can interact directly and as often as necessary. It is a pattern ubiquitous throughout Central Africa, somewhat attenuated in the South Asian syntheses, and common again throughout East Asia and Oceania. Included with this pattern is the feeding of the dead and the living sharing the food, and the use of alcohol, possibly one of the stimuli for the development of horticulture, that seems to ease attaining possession trance. (Experienced mediums, especially women, have little need of any stimulus to go into possession trance, and the equivalent is true of female shamans.) Two consequences arise from this complex. First, the family, as discussed above, becomes a socioreligious entity not simply of the present but of past and future as well. Second, this complex conception of family allows for a notion of kingship that is organic to the perception of society as a larger family.

The Chinese emperor sacrifices not only to the cosmic couple Sky-Earth, but to the human couples that are the progenitor of himself and his clan. The emperor sacrifices to his parents, grandparents and founding figures of the clan, as do all Chinese following Chinese custom. But his sacrifice is also a state sacrifice, for the imperial ancestors are more powerful than the spirits of other human dead, having been the most powerful of humans while alive. Their intercession with the deities is important not only for the ruling clan but the people as a whole. When another clan conquered the ruling clan, its first act to cement its military victory was to pull down the conquered ruler's clan temple. Mediumship was so important in these regards that mediums were Chinese court officials until about twelve hundred years ago, and the last dynasty brought the practice back. Perhaps the increasing patriarchalization of Chinese culture led to the dismissal of the court mediums, since, as everywhere in the world, mediums tend to be female. These mediums were the only females with official titles, indeed, the only females with public functions. We will return to this aspect in the next chapter.

Kingship in Central Africa is little different. Among the Asante and Akan, as examples, the soul, the power, of deceased male and female kings, who have different leadership functions, resides in blackened stools which serve as royal thrones and receive regular offerings of food and alcohol. Again, specialists, usually women, allow themselves to be possessed by the spirits of the dead rulers when communication with them is sought.

It is not just the family dead that may be sought for advice, but deceased advisors as well. The Bible contains a story in this regard that is so precise in its description of spirit possession that it must be integrating the record of an actual incident from the past. Saul, the first Israelite king, is being militarily hard pressed by his enemies, but his advisor has died. He asks a retainer where he can find a female medium and is directed to one. He goes to her in order to speak to Samuel. The Hebrew language of the Bible is very clear that it is Samuel who speaks through the mouth of the possessed medium, not the woman herself. In the following chapter, the discussion of spirit possession will continue with regard to deities.

CHAPTER FIVE

DIVINE GHOSTS:
FUNCTIONAL DEITIES

❖

The death of both my parents were due to an epidemic.
I suffered and grieved with a resentment at this injustice that
*   cut to the bone.*
As long as they lived their loving support never faltered,
On diverging paths in the worlds of light and darkness, I
*   could not give vent to my fury.*
Divine troops seized the fiends and appeared in a bright light,
The perfected being who transmitted the rite and register had
*   come in a dream.*
My brush alit and wrote a charm, saving the people from
*   ailments.*
How could I permit the five demons to tarry for even a
*   moment?*

—Terry F. Kleeman, *A God's Own Tale*

What happens to the dead that are not cared for by family?
What happens to the dead of those whose lives were important
to those outside of their own families? How do deities become
deities? In this chapter, we will explore the most common form
of deities worldwide, those in human form.

The Anthropomorphizing of the Divine

Christians will hardly find deities in human form unusual. The God of the Hebrew Bible (the Christian Old Testament) is most commonly described as exhibiting a panoply of human emotions and attitudes. For Christians, this was insufficient. Their God caused a human woman to give birth to a male who in essence, in most Christian theologies, is "fully human and fully divine."

For foraging peoples, the divine may at times appear in visions in human form to enhance communication, but when met in ordinary consciousness, they are animals, plants, natural objects, sky phenomena, and so on. In Native North America, for example, Deer or Bison may appear, at least to males, in the form of a young woman, but she remains a theriomorphic spirit.

With agriculture, people live in larger and larger villages and eventually in urban areas. The world around them is predominantly human or artificial, either crowded towns or large agricultural fields. The cosmic and nature deities come to be conceived in human form. We see this in Mayan culture: Earth, for example, is depicted as an old woman (Ixchel) in her healing and generative aspect. In the last chapter, we noted that Fox is portrayed in human form in Manchuria. Among some Native American healers that I know, those primarily residing in urban areas, their assisting spirits are dead humans. Although I was raised in a city and have continually studied or taught in urban universities, my anomalous experiences as a youth are probably responsible for my being more attuned to natural divinities than anthropomorphic ones—a most anachronistic mindset nowadays.

In China, well over two millennia in the past, the cosmic deities were reconceived in the popular mind, as elsewhere, anthropomorphically. The most important deity in this regard was the very popular King Mother of the West (incorrectly translated in the literature as the "Queen Mother of the West"). She is linked to Earth, as she resides in a cave, and is associated with the direction of the setting sun and with the mythic mountain, Kunlun, also in the west. But she is also linked to creation through spinning. Spinning in many traditions is connected to creation via Spider and web making. Although much has been written about her, she is not presently the focus of worship; thus, having no experience with her, I cannot actually understand her import and meaning. Other deities, if not fully anthropomorphic, are part human. The creator deity, Nüwa, together with her brother-spouse, Fuxi (the two were originally independent deities), are portrayed, when together, as having human upper bodies with serpent lower bodies intertwined. East and Northeast Asia are replete with a host of bird- or animal-headed, human-bodied or human-headed animal or bird-bodied deities, as, for example, my wife's natal clan's originating ancestor, mentioned in the preceding chapter.

About a thousand years ago in China a transformation occurred and the deities came to be understood as deceased humans. Cosmic and nature deities, such as the still reverenced Bixia Yuanjun (the deity of Mount Tai, discussed in the preceding chapter), were given a human biography, or deceased humans, such as Miaoshan who becomes Guanyin, were divinized. This religious transformation is, to date, little understood, although the process of divinization is relatively clear. Miaoshan, for example, is one of the human biographies attached to Guanyin, the most ubiquitous deity throughout China as a whole. Guanyin came to China from India as the male boddhisattva Avalokiteśvara, but at this time of religious change, he became a female deity. It was at this time that the female deities Bixia Yuanjun and Mazu, to be discussed below, also became popular.

Even as a male boddhisattva, Guanyin, as all bodhisattvas, is human. But Guanyin, as a divinized dead female human, is more than human. The understanding is far closer to the Chinese concept of the power of ancestral spirits, especially those of deceased rulers, than the Buddhist understanding. She seems to have replaced at least the western directional attribute of the King Mother of the West, for among her many attributes, she can help the dead reach the Western Paradise. The Western Paradise is the Pure Land of that strain of Buddhism, reinterpreted through Chinese religious filters, that is the predominant form of Buddhism in East Asia. No longer a way station for the attainment of enlightenment, it became a relatively permanent, pleasant abode for the dead in the West, the direction of the daily death of Sun, replacing the more traditional, not so pleasant underworld realm of the dead. Guanyin is also a fertility deity, as are Bixia Yuanjun and Nüwa, with regard to the ever crucial birth of male heirs to continue the patrilineal family line, and a deity worshiped by merchants.

Mazu, as a divinity, started among fishing families and maritime merchants along China's southeast coast and eventually achieved national recognition. As Taiwan was colonized by Chinese from that region, she remains the most important deity in Taiwan and southeastern China.

Both Guanyin and Mazu, as humans, were unmarried females. Both resisted marriage against their families' strong wishes, and both, in different ways, saved members of their families. They were both unfilial in disobeying their families with regard to marriage, yet exemplified filiality in saving the lives of their fathers and brothers, filial piety being the most important Chinese virtue.

Two thousand years ago, among the elite, an unmarried female was buried by her natal family, and her spirit was cared for by them. But by a thousand years ago, the patriarchalization of Chinese culture had increased. A female was not considered ever to be a part of her natal family; she belonged to the family into which she would marry. Unmarried, she belonged to no family, and there was no family to care for her if she died before, at least, betrothal. Not cared for, she would become a wandering ghost.

As in all human cultures, ghosts are not creatures one wants to come across. They have a nasty penchant for possessing people and doing other mischief. And who can blame them, being forced to continue a miserable existence. Chinese culture, as virtually all systematized cultures, has an annual festival focused on ghosts. Perhaps the best known today is Mexico's, extending from Mesoamerican Native practices. Halloween is a secularized modern Western version of the European rendition of this ubiquitous festival. In the Chinese version, originally stimulated by a Buddhist festival, ghosts wander freely for a moon (lunar month). On the day when they are most likely to be around, the middle of this month, people make offerings to these ghosts. Different from normal offerings, they are placed on a table outside of the house, along with a wash basin and a towel. The food and drink offered are more of a snack than a cooked meal. The food and drink are left in their packages or bottles. These unwelcome guests are certainly not wanted inside the home; hopefully, after washing themselves, they will just take the packaged food and wine with them and consume it elsewhere. This is the time that entertainment is put on at graveyards. Maybe the dead will enjoy the operas and remain there.

Once, residing in Taiwan near a graveyard, I heard opera being played at a distance and walked over to the source of the music, expecting to see the usual crowds. Instead, I found I was approaching the local graveyard where loudspeakers were facing the graves. I was the only living human in sight. Needless to add, I quickly left.

Parents of deceased unmarried girls, out of love for them, so that they will not become wandering ghosts, will advertise for a husband for them: a groom for a spirit marriage. Usually, a male who responds, if one can be found, will already be married and in desperate need of funds. The deceased girl will become a secondary wife. The wedding involves an eerie combination of wedding fertility and funeral death symbolism. The bridal procession, the bride encoffined, will go directly to the groom's family grave site. Her name tablet will be placed on the altar of her husband's family, to receive the same offerings as other family members.

An important function of religious specialists is to exorcize those possessed by wandering ghosts. But sometimes a possessing ghost is benign and does good things for people. People make offerings to the spirit in return. A small shrine will be built. If benefits continue to flow, the shrine will become a temple. As the benefits spread, the temple will become larger; subsidiary temples will be raised elsewhere along with the new deity's spreading fame. The government, to avoid potential disturbances, may co-opt the deity by providing titles. Mazu, for example, was given ever grander titles by the government, eventually, several hundred years ago, being bestowed with the highest honor, Empress of Sky, although she remained a sea-earth deity. This is how ghosts become deities and, probably, in essence, how most anthropomorphic deities everywhere became such.

While the most popular deities are females, all unmarried, there are, of course, many important male deities as well. Well-known magistrates and successful generals may become protecting deities of justice and of cities respectfully. Most recently, sometime in the late 1980s, with the shift to a capitalist economic environment, a new deity of wealth was needed, one that would be effective in the new economy. Who was the most powerful dead not yet with a divine specialization? Why, Mao Zedong (Mao Tse-tung), of course! Small icons of his image, with a plastic version of a Chinese gold ingot hanging from it, were on sale everywhere. They were variously hung, such as from automobile rearview mirrors, including government vehicles. When I asked a bureaucrat, a member of the Communist Party, why it was hanging there, the answer was succinct: "Ta shi shen" (He's a Deity). It is hard to imagine a greater transformation than the most important Chinese Communist ever when alive becoming, on death, a divine aid for the amassing of capitalist wealth. The deities are certainly beyond our ken.

In summary, all the spirits of the dead have power which may be used for human good or ill. This is the understanding of many traditions. In China, as in sub-Saharan Africa, most spirits are ancestral, cared for by family and benefitting family. Some are regal, the spirits of dead rulers, who are the essence of a living ruler's power. Others, not cared for, being hungry and unhappy, wander the earth, a potential danger for the living. But some of these spirits are beneficent. These and other spirits of those powerful when alive may become deities. It is understood in China, Africa, and many other areas that the deities are dead humans. To bring this back to Western culture, so are saints.

Modes of Interaction

How do we know the deities? With a host of deities, how can we tell with which one we are involved? How can they help us? How can we let them know of our needs?

In monotheism, the mode of communication is prophecy. God speaks directly to an individual or delivers via an angel His message for humans, or, as incarnated into human form, speaks directly to humans—in this case, but once only. In all three traditions, this communication is understood to be of the past, save for the mystical aspects. For Judaism, the possibility of prophecy ended with the destruction of the second temple; only the Messiah is awaited for the rebuilding of the Jerusalem temple. For Christians, direct communication ended with the execution of Jesus and his few brief postrebirth appearances to Mary Magdalene and the Disciples. For Moslems, Mohammed was the final prophet; members of the Bahai sect are executed by some Islamic governments for accepting a later prophet. All three traditions have aspects which allow for individuals to perceive or contact deity or be possessed by the Holy Spirit, all in ecstatic states, but these aspects are not universally accepted in the traditions as a whole and are looked upon askance by many.

Other traditions extend possession by family and ancestral spirits to anthropomorphic deities in general. As described in the preceding chapter, possession by the family dead is usually desirable and sought through various means, including the use of alcohol. Possession by strangers is another matter. Often the initial possession is involuntary; exorcism may be sought to remove the intruding spirit. Only if the possession proves positive for the community is it considered desirable, although it may be desired by the community but not the one possessed. We do not readily give up our bodies for strangers to use.

But those possessed may have no choice, especially if the community is in favor of the possession so that exorcism is not on the menu. Those resisting possession may become sick, and the only remedy is to allow the possession to take place. For others, often socially marginal, possession is a means to gain a degree of social recognition, although it is the deity that receives the gratitude for benefits received, not the medium. For others again, oriented toward compassion or ethical behavior, this is a wonderful opportunity to serve people, in spite of the cost to themselves. In cultures, such as African and African-influenced ones, where to be a medium is socially lauded, to be possessed may fulfill a desire to become one of the human foci of religious rituals. Finally, in families that traditionally make their living or add to their other income by

serving as mediums, this may be a family occupational tradition. The motivations and means are numerous.

In the African and African-influenced traditions where
being a medium is an honorable role, or in those in which the
role is a family tradition, mediums will undergo lengthy training. In effect, they are learning priestly as well as mediumistic
roles. In the African traditions, they must learn considerable
detail about the deities which possess them from instructors
who will be their superiors in the rituals during which they will
be possessed. There will be special behavior and distinctive
apparatus to use emblematic of the deity; they will learn the
deities' habits, voice, preferences, abilities, and so on.

In China, possession tends to be more spontaneous,
although this is not always the case. Most mediums, worldwide,
are female, but sex differences are variable, so that males also
can be spontaneously possessed. Chinese, African, African
Brazilian and African Caribbean mediums, female and male, all
agree that females are more empathetic and more open to spiritual experiences, both attributes enhancing the possibilities of
possession. (Current DNA research suggests that the difference
may indeed be in the genes.) In China, for the last several hundred years until but a decade and a half ago, females were forbidden all public roles, including mediumistic ones. Males alone
continued the tradition, at least in public. On the whole, from
my experience and observations, it seems much harder for
males in general to achieve possession trance than females,
albeit there are always exceptions to this generalization. This
may account for the differences ascribed to the different types of
mediums to be discussed in the following.

One type of Chinese medium, the predominant form since
women were forbidden to so act publicly until very recently, is a
male (there are now a few females functioning in this mode)
who in the initial phase of the trance strikes his back with a
sharp sword, a spiked ball on a rope, or the spines of a sword-
fish bill. Some will also put skewers through their biceps or
cheeks. Only a few drops of blood will appear; the bleeding
stopping almost instantaneously. A similar somatic response can
be developed by hypnotists in their subjects. It is unclear
whether this practice primarily is to engender trance through

the release of endorphins or to indicate trance to the worshippers. It is not an activity that people readily choose, unless it is a family occupation. The first Chinese medium I met, a number of years ago, was an old man living in the vicinity of my wife's parents. His clients tended to be business executives who came from a distance to consult the deities who possessed him. He himself received modest fees and was living in near poverty.

The educated elite also function as mediums but, given the Chinese focus on writing as sacred communication from as far back as we can trace Chinese writing over three millennia ago, do so in a literary manner. Spirit ("automatic") writing, writing in trance, itself can be traced back over fifteen hundred years in China. This mode of writing became the basis of what is considered the most aesthetic form of writing, itself the foundation of Chinese aesthetics as a whole. Hence, spirit writing has been extremely influential in the history of Chinese culture.

There are two contemporary modes of the educated so functioning, each with a long history. In one, a possessed person writes with a forked stick on sand in a box on a table. At least two auditors have to agree on the character so written. In this way deities write books about themselves and admonish humans to live correct, ethical lives. There are thousands of such books, and they are still being produced in large numbers. Chinese religion is the only one of which I am aware in which we have written autobiographies, not mythologies, of the deities, as in the excerpt quoted at the beginning of this chapter. A related form is connected to healing. Patients write out their needs, and the deity, through a possessed person, taps out the answer (Chinese characters depend on a number of strokes in a specific order), which is similarly read. The deity's response is copied and handed to the patient. Sometimes the deity will strike an inked seal on sacred paper, which can then be burned, the ashes mixed with water to be drunk as a medicine, or the paper is folded and worn as an amulet. Those I have met involved in these practices include university deans and bank vice presidents.

There is a related mode of interaction carried out by the illiterate or semiliterate. A miniature chair with a container for stick incense in the seat is held by two individuals. When the incense on the seat is lit, a deity is sitting there. The chair moves about, becoming lowered over sacred paper. Attached to a leg of the chair is a writing brush. The brush traces out sacred writing which is then used in the ways described above. Or a leg of the chair may tap out the characters as mentioned above.

Since the end of martial law in Taiwan and the relaxation of the ban on religious practices on the Mainland, another type of medium has come to the fore. Within a year after the end of martial law, a society of mediums was formed, at the instigation of the government, with a membership then of over two thousand. The vast majority of these members were women. Several hundred years of suppression seems not to have eradicated a traditional female activity. These mediums do not beat themselves, and they go instantly into trance. They serve as mediums for healing and related purposes for no fee; indeed, the travel they undergo and other expenses can be a drain on family income.

Some of these possessions can be almost unbelievable. While researching these mediums and their society several years ago, I was taken to an outlying large new temple where several types of mediumistic healing were taking place in different parts of the temple simultaneously. One medium was famous for her possessing deity healing from four to six hundred people each of the two days a week she did this, each diagnosis and healing taking from but one to two minutes. So many people came that a volunteer orchestra played traditional instruments to entertain the waiting lines, television monitors were set up to play videos of temple-sponsored pilgrimages, and an excellent multicourse free lunch for hundreds was put on at midday.

As I was talking in the office with the temple founder and administrators, I was taken, I thought, to observe her at work up close. Instead I was put at the head of the line. I was instantly diagnosed: first, I was told that I had a problem with my heart related to my blood—at the time I had just started taking, on doctor's orders, a cholesterol-reducing drug, and I had told no one in Taiwan about it. Second, I was told that my work was being blocked—since I was an academic, there would be many ways to see that happening. I was told that this blockage would be taken care of or something to that effect. The whole event took fewer than ninety seconds, and, as this was entirely unexpected, I was not prepared for precision in remembering the exact words.

At lunch, I sat at the same table as the medium, and it was quite apparent that she had no memory, as is usually the case, not only of my healing but of me, and as a bearded Caucasian, I certainly stood out from anyone else healed that morning.

On returning from Taiwan, I found a letter waiting for me at my office that had been mailed the day before I left by a person who knew my flight dates. This letter cancelled an accepted publication, an issue of a religious studies journal, that had already been advertised with its table of contents. It was an anthology on female spirituality for which I was responsible and included the work of many scholars. I had been warned by a colleague who attempted unethical action that I refused to endorse that she would have revenge, but I hardly expected anything like this. As this was the journal of a scholarly society of which I was president and the executive refused to intervene, out of responsibility with regard to the insult of this action to the many affected scholars I had brought into the society, I had no choice but to resign my office. Obviously, the deity was aware of the decision announced by the letter long before I was.

Several months later, when my courses ended and I could get back to the book on female spirituality which I was writing, something very strange happened. What I had assumed would take me two to three more years I accomplished in a month and a half. I was writing a chapter a week, frequently driving back to my office in the city for more and more references. I could scarcely believe what was happening. Not only was the diagnosis absolutely correct but the healing was beyond any expected effectiveness. But that was not all. Within a few months of completing the first draft, I had found a publisher, and it was out within a year. Those familiar with academic publishing will know that this is quite unusual. My previous book had bounced around among publishers for a number of years before acceptance. I had witnessed obvious cases of immediate physical healing by deities through spirit possession, but this was the first time I was directly affected. Because I was attuned to nature and cosmic spirits rather than anthropomorphic ones, I had been at a personal distance from what I had been observing with regard to mediumism (not with the wonderful mediums). No longer.

At the same time, my work on the society of mediums received similar support, which I assume is the work of the Dragon King deity of their head temple. I received a very short-term grant, funded by the Taiwan Ministry of Education, to study the society, a study with which the society fully cooperated. I finished the paper while still in Taiwan. In less than a year from its completion, I presented the paper at the annual meeting of the American Academy of Religion, and it was in print in a refereed journal. All of my many previous journal publications took years to be accepted and years more to come out in print (one journal article was accepted for publication over twenty-five years ago and has yet to be published).

This is not to imply that all mediums are selfless or effective containers for the deities. I have been with purported mediums who were more fooling themselves than anyone else as to their possession. And I have witnessed charlatans. But then I have little sympathy for those who go to commercial temples to receive winning lottery numbers from the deities through spirit possession. These private storefront temples have sprung up with the inception of state-run lotteries in Taiwan, often selling the tickets along with supposed divine advice on the winning numbers.

This is a book on theology, not mediumism. The above discourse is about one major way deities interact with humans, not the mediums themselves, about whom much more could be said. As with shamans, mediums are but a means for the deities to assist humans. Those within such traditions do not thank the human involved but the deity responsible for helping them. Of course, the community will appreciate, to varying degrees, the effort of the human facilitating the deity's activities.

But spirit possession is not the ordinary means for interaction with the deities. With few exceptions, the common means is one universal to human cultures with anthropomorphic deities: reverence and requests using images of the deities as a focal point. Judaism and Islam have an aversion to the use of images as a focus for worship; both substitute for images a book that is understood as sacred in and of itself and treated accordingly. But surely the imparting of long, complex texts in human language by God or through angels is evidence of anthropomorphism. Christianity theoretically does not worship images and understands all traditions outside of the Religions of the Book to be idolatrous. We can readily understand the confusion of the Chinese who were told by Catholic missionaries that their religious practices were idolatrous and, therefore, to be utterly eradicated and then were taught to offer candles to and pray before images of Mary and the saints just as they did to the images of the Chinese deities (candles are a ubiquitous offering in Chinese temples).

Chinese family altars, different from clan altars, are complex. Usually, on the wall over the altar will be a two-dimensional image of Guanyin. The tablets with the names of the family dead will be on the left side of the altar for those facing it. In the middle will be a small statue of a deity usually linked to the primary occupation of the primary male of the family; Guanyin tends to be worshiped by the primary female and other females of the family. On the right, there may be another image of, or sacred paraphernalia belonging to, a deity that has a special relationship with someone in the family. Hence, there will be two or three sets of offering furnishings, with daily offerings made with each set.

Traditionally, every village and urban neighborhood has a temple. The temple grounds will be the only public space in the community. There is no clergy; the temple is administered by a neighborhood or village committee. Here is where public meetings will be held, where public entertainment—nominally for the deities housed there—will take place, where older people hang out, where children play, where local people gather in the evening to play musical instruments or chess, and where grain may be dried at harvest time. The temple building will theoretically focus on one or a few deities, but anyone is free to contribute an image, and over time, the temple will be crowded with a multitude of images. All will be worshipped.

On major offering days, people, usually women, will bring the uncooked food for the sacrificial meal to the temple to be offered to the deities housed there and then bring the food home to be cooked and offered as a banquet before the family altar, before the family themselves eat the food. If the local temple is on the route home from the local market, the food may be offered to the deities in the temple before being brought home every time one goes shopping, which, before the availability of refrigeration, was daily. For special purposes, people will travel, sometimes long distances, to temples whose deities are known to be especially efficacious for particular needs. During the examinations for university entrance in Taiwan, where there are far more applicants than places, certain temples are crowded with supplicating high school students.

These images are not simply representative of the deities any more than Catholic or Orthodox Christian images are. Pope John-Paul did not have to leave Rome to go the Black Madonna in Poland simply to worship Mary; Rome is hardly lacking in images of her. Perhaps a good indication of the living element of the images is that in Taiwan, television sets are so placed in local temples so that they can comfortably be seen by the statues of the deities, rendering them difficult for humans to see. Obviously, time and money would not have been spent if there was no one to watch the programs.

On the other hand, nowhere, of course, is there an idol that is understood to be a deity in and of itself. The whole point of a representative image is exactly that. Hence, Christianity is not against idols; it is against any others than its own. For a Christian to label a non-Christian as an idolater, unless it is a Protestant doing so, is nonsensical. And for that matter, is not the Torah treated exactly as is an image in many other traditions? In the synagogue, the Torah is housed in a special shrine. It is dressed in rich vestments, and a silver crown and other ornaments are placed on it. When it is removed from its resting placed and undressed, it is done so ritually. It is paraded around the synagogue and the congregation surges forward to touch and kiss it. I have witnessed the same behavior with regard to images in many cultures, including Roman Catholic ones.

It is not sufficient for an image simply to be manufactured; it must be spiritually charged, so that it embodies a degree of the spiritual power of the deity. In China, one image, often considered to be the oldest, will serve as the main charging station; other older images will serve as subsidiary home temples. Images from temples and homes will be placed in the vicinity of these powerful images for a period of time. The images become related to each other as family; all, of course, embodying some power of and a connection to the actual deity. On the deity's birthday, they often travel in a grand procession to the mother temple, with the image carried in a sedan chair. This has been related to the traditional yearly return to their natal home by women (now, of course, women in Taiwan simply jump into their car and drive to their natal home whenever they wish). The images are accompanied by the local mediums whom the deity possesses. As the chair reaches the vicinity of the mother temple, the deity becomes excited and the chair jumps about; the chair bearers carry it forward with great difficulty. At the temple, the deity enters the bodies of the mediums and is available for healing (in the broad sense). About fifteen years ago, tens of thousands of people from Taiwan crossed the rough strait in small fishing boats, against the direct orders of the Taiwan government, to the mainland to recharge their images of Mazu at the primary Mazu temple in Fujian Province. Now they are carried back and forth by airplane.

There are many ways anthropomorphic deities relate to people. The two discussed above are but very common means. There are, of course, many others as well, such as dreams, visions, pilgrimages, and so on. For if the deities and humans did not interrelate, the concept of, as well as the reality of, deity would have no meaning.

CHAPTER SIX

THE SEMINUMINOUS: CULTURE HEROES AND TRICKSTERS

❖

He planted (the soil) with large beans;
The beans waved (in the wind).
The cultivated grain had plenty of ears:
The hemp [for clothes] and grain grew thickly.
The gourd stems bore ample fruit.
The Lord of Millet's husbandry
Followed the method of assisting (the plants).
He cleared away the wild grass;
He sowed it with the yellow riches [millet];
It grew evenly and luxuriantly.
It was thick; it was tall;
It flowered and set ears;
It became firm and good;
It had ripe ears; it had solid kernels.

—From the *Odes* in Jordan Paper & Lawrence G. Thompson, *The Chinese Way in Religion*

[Exú] is the guardian of the ground and opener of paths . . . the intermediary between human beings and the gods, and master of the shells we use for divining. . . . Everybody knows that he's a jokester, a gambler and a drinker, that he chases after women. . . . Exú's also the god of fertility and fecundity. A long time ago he used to be shown . . . with a huge erect penis. . . . [H]e

*has a tendency to be an exhibitionist.... Also, his language
isn't very clean.... He often expresses himself with "dirty"
words. Sometimes he pinches the pretty girls in the audience
and makes all kinds of unsolicited remarks, puns and obscene
gestures.*

—Maria-José in Serge Bramely, *Macumba*

Because of the role of sacred texts in the Religions of the Book
and in South Asia, there is a general assumption in the West that
myths describe functional deities; that is, deities to whom we
make requests. Furthermore, it is assumed that myths are the
foundations of rituals. Christian ritual, to a very limited degree,
involves the acting out of myths found in the Gospels, following
the pattern of many Hellenistic mystery rituals, and this particular relationship between myth and ritual is assumed the norm
for religion in general. The addition of writing leads to the further assumption that these myths are fixed, unchanging over
time. But none of the traditions discussed in the preceding chapters have such texts.

It is the case for China that writing in and of itself is considered sacred, as writing from its very beginnings has been used
for communication with the spirit realm and, as well, remains a
major method of communication by the divine to humans as
discussed in the preceding chapters. And in China, there are
Buddhist, Daoist, and *rujia* (the ideology of the civil service
examination system, invariably mistranslated as "Confucian-
ism") sets of texts. But these are all tangential to normative Chinese religion as described in chapters 4 and 5.

In sub-Saharan Africa, Native America, and East Asia, the
mythic tales told are, in the main, unrelated to rituals. They tend
to narrate stories of numinous and seminuminous beings,
termed in the religious studies literature "culture heroes," those
beings that provide humans with the tools and skills for living,
and "tricksters," beings that do not fit the Western expectations
of pious behavior on the part of the divine. In many cultures, the
two aspects are part and parcel of the same entities. Until the
influence of Western literature and drama, these mythic tales

formed the core of popular entertainment: storytelling and drama. In Chinese culture, these tales continue in films and in television series. Hence, popular entertainment contained both pedagogical and sacred functions, maintaining the lack of separation between sacred and secular in all modes of human endeavor. Obviously, these myths are not fixed but continually vary according to inspiration, as discussed in chapter 3, or as told by the deities themselves, as discussed in chapter 5.

Numinous Beings Unconnected to Rituals

Aside from legends, tales about important humans of the past and the basis of historical understanding, the most common stories told in Native American traditions are myths. These myths are tales about the numinous and the basis of religiocultural understanding; they are about divinities and spirits who impart to humans the essentials of culture and civilization: culture heroes. In northern North America, these numinous beings are in animal form, but being shape shifters, they can change into the form of any entity, including trees and rocks, as well as humans. Most common are Hare, Coyote, Raven, and Spider, who in the southwest of the United States is also a clan deity.

Many of these figures, for example, Hare and Spider, are also common in Africa, and in the southeast of the United States, during the period of slavery, Native American and African myths coalesced into such tales as those concerning Br'er Rabbit. Hollywood cartoonists picked up on these images and turned them into very successful animated cartoons. Their success may well be due to providing, in a monotheistic culture, an opportunity to share the combined humor and wisdom inherent to these stories. Bugs Bunny, Coyote, and the jive-talking "Negro" crows in *Dumbo* are all modifications of these mythic foci, derived from the culture heroes of differing Native American traditions.

Throughout the Algonkian language cultures of northeast and central North America, this figure is Nanabush (or Nanabozo and other dialectical variants). The major myth cycles focus on him, and his most common form, when not human, is as a hare. One of the early Jesuit missionaries accordingly

assumed that the sole deity of these people was a "Great Hare."
Other than in a modified form in the Midéwiwin initiation rituals, a *cultus* (in the original Hellenistic meaning) within Anishnabe religion, there are no rituals or offerings relevant to him.
There are many mythic versions. What follows is extracted from
the ones with which I happen to be most familiar.

Typical of, but not necessary to, culture heroes, Nanabush is
part human and part deity. He is borne by Beautiful Woman: a
human female, yet linked to Earth, who was impregnated by
West Wind (see chapter 2). She dies in childbirth, and he is
raised by Grandmother, who too is human but linked to Moon,
and, in some versions, she is Moon. When he was an infant, to
protect him at a time of danger, his grandmother placed a bowl
over him, and he changed into a hare in order to survive by
eating the grass under the bowl. Over the course of his growth
into a mature adult, he brings his grandmother and the human
community in which she resides many cultural artifacts and
necessities, including fire, which, as in many traditions worldwide, he steals from other beings. Books of translated myths are
available about him, and it is not possible, in a short space, even
to hint at the many deeds attributed to him and stories about
him. He is central to the recreation of the world, a theme to
which we shall return in this chapter.

Aside from the many important gifts Nanabush brings, he is
also mischievous and an asinine fool. Primarily he fools himself.
The stories illustrate the absurd situations to which pride, anger,
and so on can lead. The stories, termed in the religious studies
literature "trickster tales," tell not just how the world came to be
and how culture developed, but how we as humans should live
and act. Typical of Native cultures, we do not make fun of others
in providing illustrations but of ourselves. In his foolishness,
Nanabush ends up harming himself rather than others. These
stories made up the entertainment for the long winter nights.
Nonetheless, they are sacred tales and can be told only in their
proper ritual time (the above brief outline is not a myth per se),
from the first appearance of Snow until the coming of first
Thunder, that is, from late autumn to early spring.

Coyote (Oldman) is the major figure in the Plains. Even
more than Nanabush, he gets himself into the most absurd situa-

tions; in one story, he ends up cooking and eating his own anus, after being tricked by Fox and Raccoon. In another story, he repeatedly insists that his penis acknowledge the wonderful, fat bison bull he spied. Finally, his penis does verbally note the bison and then, to Coyote's dismay, refuses to shut up, repeating the acknowledgment over and over again. Those who could not wait for their first child to speak and then, subsequently, wished the child would shut up will empathize with this story.

Many of the stories are scatological, often in impossible, ridiculous ways, but some realistically. Most translations are heavily expurgated, thus losing the wonderful humor and flavor of these tales. I did not understand their purpose until I began telling them to my children when they were quite young. Although they had just learned to read, they latched on to the book that was the source of many of the stories, written in adult language, and read them repeatedly until the book fell apart. They learned the tales verbatim and told them to each other over and over again, correcting any errors in oral transmission. No other stories grabbed them even near to the same extent. The reason for this style of myth came to me: children love scatological humor. That element of the myths was deliberate, a pedagogical device to ensure that children learned in detail these tales of proper and improper behavior.

Raven is important in Northwest Coast cultures, from northern California to the Alaskan panhandle, and figures in stories of the origin of humans and the temporary stealing of the sun. What is fascinating about Raven, from a comparative perspective, is that these stories seem to have traveled around the Pacific, since an identical one, the archery shooting of multiple suns leaving but one, is found in both northern California and coastal China.

Shape-shifting beings are found elsewhere, often termed "were beings." In East Asia, the most common are Fox and Snake. In China and further north, they take can take on the form of beautiful women and seduce young men. Often they are benign and can lead to great success for the family, unless their true identity is discovered, in which case they, and possibly the resultant children, will disappear (a theme found in Hellenic myths and many other traditions). Others are maleficent and lead to death and destruction unless exorcized. In Manchuria, the fox deity, portrayed in human guise, is a ubiquitous sacred image in homes (although hidden from nonfamily eyes given the communist regime). In Japan, the sexual orientation tends to be reversed. The fox spirits are handsome males that seduce young women. But in Japan, different from China, elite women had sexual freedom until the second wave of cultural borrowing from China in the twelfth century. In China, the story of the White Snake, a female spirit who marries a man in a variation of the above plot, is a major theme in traditional popular literature and operas.

These stories also exist in the West, but due to monotheism, these beings cannot be accepted as numinous, unless the connotation is utterly evil. Hence, they are relegated to fantastic horror stories, or the tales are connected with the Devil and considered Satanic. Tales of wonder and humor thus are separated from religious understanding. We are not prepared to see Bugs Bunny as a divine being, although he certainly engenders sublime laughter. Nor do we laugh during our religious ceremonies. Many times I have observed Native elders in the midst of ceremonies tell a joke when they felt the mood had become too somber. Humor is as important an aspect of the sacred to them as any other. Life without humor is not only inhuman; it is ungodly.

Trickster and Humorous Divinities

But trickster figures can also be deities in the Western concept of divinity as well. They must be treated with great care and never neglected, for the tricks they can play on us can be disastrous. Yet, if they wish, they can be of enormous help as well.

The ceremonies of Candomblé, the African Brazilian religion centered in Bahia, begin with a ritual offering outside of the ceremonial grounds to Exú, a trickster deity who must be placated before the main rituals begin. Exú can appear in many modes. In the African Brazilian and African Caribbean religions, due to the required adherence to Catholicism in the French, Spanish, and Portuguese colonies, the African deities were paired with Christian saints and other sacred personages. Exú as the opener of sacred paths is paired with St. Peter, but as being available for black (negative) sorcery, he is paired with Satan, and as intermediary between humans and the other deities, as well as master of the divining shells, he is paired with the angel Gabriel. He appears in many other modes as well. When he manifests himself in the bodies of mediums, he can be quite exuberant and unpredictable, and his language is scatological. He can facilitate or ruin a ceremony; hence, he must be appeased with the first offering. He is both loved and feared. His consort, or his female mode, depending on point of view, is a sexy seducer.

Divinities too, need not be serious and sober, as the monotheistic deity is invariably presented. Deities can be hilarious figures, jokes in and of themselves, yet be beneficent and powerful. A popular Chinese deity is Jigong. His image is of a tipsy, disheveled figure often appearing in the way the late comic Red Skeleton portrayed a farcical drunk. Yet He is one of the most powerful healing deities. According to His biography, He became a Buddhist monk in his late teens, after completing the three year's mourning for his parents (thereby not utterly violating Chinese morality in becoming a monk). Apparently an actual well-known monk while alive, Jigong was notorious for his drinking, in spite of the Buddhist prohibition against alcoholic beverages. He is also known as Ji Dien ("the Dipso-[maniac] Savior"). Jigong is particularly potent with regard to healing, settling lawsuits and vanquishing demons, using His omnipresent palm leaf fan. I first directly encountered Jigong via a possessed medium; He is quite a card. A common stunt to indicate His divine powers when He appears through mediums is to convert His own urine into wine, surely a more difficult feat than turning water into wine. As the only foreigner at this particular mediumistic seance, the gourd into which He pissed was given to me to taste to verify whether or not the deity was indeed present. It was fairly good rice wine.

Culture Hero Quasi Deities

Culture heroes, as well, may also be the recipients of ritual offerings. In the following, three types of recipients will be described: semidivine, semihuman; not divine, but fully human; and fully divine, maybe.

To return to the imperial altars in Beijing, the ones yet to be described share a large compound which includes the altars to Earth Spirits and Sky Spirits mentioned in chapter 2. These are the altars to the First Agriculturist and the First Sericulturist (one who raises silkworms and spins silk). The emperor made offerings at the former, ploughing token furrows in the spring, and the empress made offerings to the First Sericulturist and did token spinning.

The First Agriculturist, the giver of agriculture to humans, is originally described in an early sacrificial ode as the founder of the Zhou ruling clan, three millennia ago. Typical of culture heroes worldwide, He has a divine father, perhaps avian, and a human mother. As an infant He was several times abandoned and saved by animals and birds; one is reminded of the Hellenic culture hero Hercules and His trials. The name of the First Agriculturist is Houji, the Lord of Millet, millet being the early staple crop of northern China, now maize and wheat. He introduces the many kinds of grains and then the sacrificial offerings to the ancestral spirits. In essence, these offerings are to Himself, since Houji is the founding clan ancestor relevant to these sacrificial odes. For rulers of succeeding dynasties, Houji is not, of course, an ancestor; the offerings are made to him as having virtually divine status. He is, accordingly, part divine and part human, as was Hercules in Hellenistic religion.

This is different in the case of Kongzi (Master Kong—Confucius) and other literati heroes sanctified in temples to the First Teacher found in all Chinese administrative centers prior to this century (and still present in many). Because Kongzi is not divine but fully human, he can be sacrificed to only by his kin. In Taibei (Taipei), where the sacrifice on his assumed birthday is still carried on with government support, the ritual is put on by academics and students, but the sacrificer per se must be a descendant of Kongzi. It is understood, indeed found in the *Lunyü* (*Analects*) of Kongzi, that it is wrong, if not dangerous, to sacrifice to those, other than divinities, that are not one's own deceased relatives. Hence, Kongzi is a culture hero, but one that is not divine at all.

Fully human culture heroes also exist in Western traditions, even though ritual offerings are not part of the religious practices. For example, in the religion that a number of religionists term "Americanism," both George Washington and Abraham Lincoln, in all respects, function as culture heroes. An annual special day is set aside to commemorate them. Although not technically religious holidays, given the unique read in the United States of the separation of church and state to avoid having a state religion wedded to a church during the formation of the Constitution, in all other respects they are sacred days. These are public holidays (not in the Southern states for Lincoln) and special ceremonies and teachings take place in the schools. Both historic figures, related to the origination or continuation of the state, are surrounded by myths. These include stories of their childhood with no factual context, and an understanding of their accomplishments not based on historical data; for example, that Lincoln's primary purpose in fighting the Civil War was to free the slaves, rather than to deny the Southern states their assumed right to disassociate from a voluntary confederation. But these nationalistic myths are true in the same sense that religious myths are true: they are foundational stories. Both figures are celebrated in prominent monumental public buildings in the national capital that are either modeled on Greco-Roman temples or on ancient Egyptian sacred memorial pillars.

To return to China, Fuxi, mentioned in chapter 5 as the brother-spouse of Nüwa, is a culture hero, the provider to humans of, among other artifacts, fishnets and the Trigrams, essential to many forms of divination in China and considered the origin of Chinese writing. The pair are officially spoken of as the ancestors of humans, but, as is obvious from the fact that most offerings are made to Nüwa alone, she solely is understood to be the geneatrix of humans in the popular mind. Fuxi is also one the mythic Sage Emperors and has a mausoleum, with temples to him and Nüwa, in Honan Province, where there is a month-long Ancestor of Humans Festival. As mentioned before, when portrayed as a divine couple, they have human torsos and serpent bodies. Are they divine? Are they human? Here, I am afraid, our Western categories breakdown. They are certainly fully divine, yet they are our original ancestors.

In Candomblé, Ogoun is essentially a blacksmith deity, the
giver of metals and metalworking, and as discussed in chapter
3, having a sacred aura. He is the patron deity of all those who
work with metal tools. Because mediums possessed by him
wield swords as well as wrought iron implements, he is also a
warrior deity and associated with St. George, the slayer of dragons. As metal is created from ore by burning off impurities, so
Ogoun is considered incorruptible, an exemplar of purity, one
who works for justice. All cultures have a panoply of culture
heroes, a recognition that culture, in and of itself, and the con-
stituents of culture, that is, those things and activities that make
us human, have a divine nature.

Re-creation of the World versus Creation

As mentioned above, one of the major themes of the
Nanabush myth cycle is recreation of the world. It is a myth
found in many parts of the world, including in the Hebrew Bible
(the Noah theme). Indeed, it is so ubiquitous that late diffusion
is most unlikely. We may have here a myth that goes back to the
very beginnings of human culture and spread with humans
throughout this planet.

There are many variations of this Anishnabe myth cycle,
particularly regarding the instigation of the flood; some of the
present ones are clearly due to influence from Christian missionaries and their imparting of the Noah account. In many versions,
in brief outline, the underwater monster deities, angered at
Nanabush's killing of their leader (in an act of revenge for the
killing of his brother, Wolf), in turn have their revenge by causing the waters to rise (revenge is a major cause of raiding in foraging cultures). Nanabush's grandmother and the other humans
make a raft to survive the rising waters. When all the land has
disappeared, Nanabush asks various water animals and birds to
dive to the bottom to bring up some mud. The fourth one suc-
ceeds, and Nanabush spreads it to become the present surface of
the land. Thus, the land is recreated. The myth cycle begins with
the birth of Nanabush. There are already land and people prior
to the flood, as there are in the biblical version.

The influence of Christianity and awareness of Genesis led to the attachment of a Genesis-like creation myth most awkwardly to versions of this cycle, for example, that of the Lenape (Delaware). There is no smooth transition between them. Similarly, a rewritten Mayan myth cycle, created a century after the Spanish conquest by a Mayan literate in Spanish, and, hence, familiar with the Bible, prefaces the Mayan myths with a creation myth virtually identical to that found in Genesis. Western scholars, consequently, have in effect written, "Eureka, the Mayans have a creation myth just like ours." Is not proof wonderful!

In cultures where river dikes are of major importance, the role of the culture hero in the flood myth may be supplanted by the culture hero's introducing the building of dikes. The civilization that developed in northern China did so on a vast flood plain. The Huangho (Yellow River), a river with an enormous flow, after leaving the mountains runs through a very soft soil (loess) and carries considerable yellowish sediment, hence its name. The dropping sediment fills the river bed in the middle and lower reaches of the river, and without dikes, the Huangho frequently overflows, flooding a vast area. The culture hero Yü the Great completed the Huangho dikes, taking on the task of his father, after nine (a sacred number in very early China) years of unceasing effort. According to one version of the myth, he was born from a human mother who conceived after witnessing a falling star and swallowing a divine pearl. He was a faithful minister to the mythic "Sage Emperors" Yao and Shun. After the death of the latter, he became the last of the Sage Emperors and the founder of the Xia, the first semihistorical dynasty.

Creation myths are found only where they are meaningful. The Western notion of time demands one and so the Hebrew Bible was edited with relatively late creation myths placed at the beginning. And since the editors could not agree on which one to use, they chose two (but the Noah mythic element is most likely earlier). Hence, the Hebrew Bible can literally begin with the Hebrew word meaning "in the beginning." The Christian Bible completes the theme with the apocalyptic end of time in Revelations.

The Chinese do not have a cosmic creation myth, nor is there a concept of a Creator. Although an Indo-European South

Asian creation myth, in which the Creator creates the cosmos
out of Himself, became part of Chinese folklore, it does not function as a myth. What the Chinese have instead are clan-origin
myths, as discussed in chapter 4. For the clan is far more important to the clan members than the world in general. In Chinese
metaphysics, everything creates itself (*ziran*), so that a creation
myth would contradict the Chinese worldview. Among popular
myths, there are those concerning the creation of humans, as the
one relating to Nüwa mentioned above, but this is closer to clan-
origin myths than a world-creation myth. Japan has a beautiful
myth regarding the creation of the Japanese islands, but that is
because the culture is islandcentric; in any case, the islands are
created by a male-female pair of Kami (divinities—themselves
created by other Kami) in a myth with wonderful sexual allu-
sions, not by a single deity.

The point of the above is to counter the assumption central
to the monotheistic theologies, and accentuated in medieval
Christian theology with its skewed use of Aristotle's concept of
first cause, that all cultures must have a creating deity. If time
has no beginning, nor any end, there simply is no absolute
beginning or initial creation. Earth and Sky, for most cultures,
have always existed. They are deities in and of themselves. As
the Chinese said to the sixteenth- and seventeenth-century Jesuit
missionaries (see the next chapter), "Who could possibly create
Sky and Earth?"

Beginnings are relative. All traditions have origin myths, but
they need not be about the beginning of the material world.
Even in the Religions of the Book, this is not the essential beginning. For Judaism, the foundational mythic beginning is the
story of the Patriarchs, particularly the first Covenant with
Abram, who then becomes Abraham. For normative Christianity, it is the death and resurrection of Christ, not his birth. The
latter is essentially a later borrowed Mythraic myth of the birth
of Mithras, the Sun. For Islam, it is the revelation by an angel to
Mohammed of God's teachings.

Yet the first question regarding myth asked by Westerners of
other traditions is "Who is your Creator?" The answer "We
don't have one" is not acceptable. For Western scholars, this
must mean that the myth has been lost, as I was long taught by

my Western teachers regarding China, or the culture is so primitive that its members have not yet learned to think like real human beings.

Implications

We in the West tend to have a very narrow view of divinity. In ignorance of Hellenic and Hellenistic deities as they were originally understood, we have used them as a model for understanding polytheistic traditions as a whole. I use the word "ignorance" because the view of the Indo-European divinities imparted in North American schools has been so decontextualized from their religious and other cultural underpinnings that these understanding can have no possible validity.

Hence, Western culture is unaware of deities that are amusing, tricky, simultaneously benevolent and maleficent, sometimes stupid and yet all-powerful, neither divine nor human, and often a combination of these and many more traits. Examples have been illustrated above. Remnants do exist. The Book of Job begins with Satan, a virtual equal of God, gambling with Him over human faithfulness to God. With God's go-ahead, Satan inflicts on Job a panoply of horrendous events; hence, God is acting, along with Satan, in a trickster capacity. Different, however, from the polytheistic traditions described above, God is utterly callous toward human suffering. For it is not God who suffers, but humans, who are but playthings in the game between God and Satan. After God wins the bet, Job is given back what he lost, but only with regard to possessions. His children, who die in a windstorm, are utterly ignored. Instead, Job is given new sons and daughters after God wins His contest with Satan.

Western monotheism leads us to expect, if not a single deity, at least a chief deity who alone in the beginning of time creates the world. This assumes a unique understanding of time, found in no other cultural complex of which I am aware. This "bigbang" concept of beginnings, different from all but the latest modern physics theories in that it occurs but once, also differs from cyclic and "steady-state" concepts. Along with the world, human beings are created. Accordingly, the following is a frequent question of cultures unimbued with Western thinking in response to a creating deity: "Then who created God?" For the monotheistic creation in normative human thinking leads to an infinite regression, no different from the chicken-egg conundrum. Hence, other nonmonotheistic traditions focus on recreation myths, clan-origin myths, or emergence or migration myths: how we got where we are. And all of these are also reflected in the monotheistic sacred texts: respectively, the Noah story, the story of the Patriarchs, and the story of the forty-year's wandering in the desert before reaching the Holy Land. What monotheism adds is the beginning of time by a being who exists before time, requiring a leap of logic, requiring faith rather than common sense.

CHAPTER SEVEN

ONE OR MANY: MONOTHEISTS' MISPERCEPTIONS OF POLYTHEISM

❖

During the last few years, whilst interpreting their works [the Chinese Classics] with good masters, I have found many passages which are favorable to the things of our Faith, such as the unity of God, the immortality of the soul, the glory of the elect, etc.

—Matteo Ricci, S.J., 1595, in Jacques Gernet, *China and the Christian Impact*

Polytheism is Defined by Monotheism

All the interconnected monotheistic traditions define themselves, in essence, as simply not being polytheistic. At their basis, each has a creed that either states or begins with a statement that it is monotheistic; for example, the Christian Nicene creed which begins with the statement, "We believe in one God, the Father Almighty, Maker of heaven and earth." Such creeds would be nonsensical unless they were setting their adherents apart from a religio-cultural milieu in which it was assumed that deities were multiple. The Christian creed goes further than the other Religions of the Book in stipulating that the single deity is male, given that many of the competing mystery religions focused on a female deity, and it emphasizes that the single deity is the manufacturer of the cosmos, thus denying the common understanding that Sky and Earth are deities in and of themselves.

Hence, "polytheism" is a monotheistic construct. Polytheists have no reason to have a term for themselves, since polytheism is the human cultural norm. Indeed, as we will discuss in the next chapter, polytheism can be understood as reflecting human nature, the corollary being that monotheism is contrary to it. The only indispensable characteristic that polytheists of different traditions have in common is not how monotheists identify them, but the very fact that polytheists are so identified. It is the identification by monotheists that defines polytheism. Polytheists would have no more reason to call themselves such than they would to call themselves "air breathers" or "bipedal." This treatise presenting a generalized polytheistic theology makes sense only in a monotheistic cultural environment.

But polytheism is not simply a monotheistic construct, for the word relates to a set of pejorative terms; polytheists are rarely if ever simply labeled "polytheists." Rather, polytheists are termed "pagans" and "heathens" by Christians. According to the *Concise Oxford Dictionary*, a "pagan" is a "person not subscribing to any of the main religions of the world, esp. formerly regarded by Christians as unenlightened or heathen." A "heathen" is 1) "a person who does not belong to a widely-held religion (esp. who is not Christian, Jew, or Muslim) as regarded by those that do"; 2) "an unenlightened person; a person regarded as lacking culture or moral principles." Hence, a pagan or heathen is anyone who is not an adherent of one of the monotheistic traditions, with the understanding that such a person is inferior and dangerous. A polytheist is someone lacking in religion, as well as all moral and ethical sensibility. This is not an archaic understanding. In a relatively recent popular news magazine article titled "Inside China's Search for Its Soul," all references to normative Chinese religion are termed superstition; the word "religion" is primarily reserved for Christianity: "And members of China's new middle class are embracing both state-of-the-art technology to transform their economy and 5,000-year-old superstitions to support their lives" (J. A. Florcruz & J. C. Ramo, *Time* [Canadian ed.] 4 Oct 99, 55–59).

Nor are the Western sciences any more benign in their attitude toward polytheism. A term which one might have supposed would have died with the end of evolutionary and racist premises in religious studies still continues. Polytheists are frequently termed "animists," a term I have never been able to wrap my mind around. The *Concise Oxford Dictionary* defines "animism" as 1) "the attribution of a living soul to plants, inanimate objects, and natural phenomena," and 2) "the belief in a supernatural power that organizes and animates the material universe." The second definition is irrelevant to this discussion as it posits a monotheistic deity within the meaning of the term. Yet the first definition is meaningless to polytheism as it has no reference to divinity whatsoever, and it is so vague that it is useless in any other regard. But the term is still current. A recent film designed for college classroom use, *The Roots of Belief: Animism to Abraham, Moses and Buddha*, is the first of a series of ten films supposedly encompassing the entirety of human religions. According to the sales blurb, the film jumps from Neanderthals to Abraham. In this case, polytheists are not considered immoral and dangerous so much as inferior human beings, replaced in the evolution of humans by superior Christian Caucasians, similar to the replacement in Europe of Neanderthals by Homo sapiens. In summary, to admit that one is a polytheist is to damn oneself in the eyes of other members of Western cultures.

Ur-monotheism

All humans, by their very nature, are ethnocentric. We are cultural as well as social beings, and we assume ourselves, including the culture in which we operate and define ourselves, to be normal. Since in monotheistic cultures ultimate truth is singular, that focus on singularity tends to inform every type of

value as well as modes of thinking, an effect of monotheism to
which we shall return in the next chapter. Since there is only one
truth, it follows that there is only one true belief, one true religion, one true culture. Monotheism frequently demands an
extreme form of ethnocentrism. It is no longer an understanding
that one's culture is normal, nor even that all other cultures are
inferior; monotheism has often led to an understanding that all
other cultures are wrong and the enemy of the one true culture.
Nevertheless, liberal strains within the monotheistic traditions
tend to resist this absolutism, and some are overtly tolerant.

This understanding of singularity affects all Western intellectual endeavors, including religious studies. From the beginnings of the study of non-Western religions by the Jesuit
missionaries in the sixteenth century, religion has been understood in an evolutionary sense, long before Darwin applied the
concept to zoological observation. It was assumed that cultures
move from polytheism to monotheism to Christianity. But this
notion implied a developmental truth which was at odds with
understanding Truth to be absolute, even through time. Hence,
there arose an early concept of ur-monotheism, to be more fully
developed in the late nineteenth and early twentieth centuries.
The earliest cultures were understood to have been monotheistic
but lost the Truth, until it was rediscovered by the Israelites and
fulfilled by Christ. It was a revision of the "Adam and Eve and
the Fall" story, of "Paradise Lost."

Polytheistic religions were understood not simply to be
wrong; polytheism was indicative of nonhuman status. Islam
early included limited toleration for Jews and Christians, for the
other "Peoples of the Book," but for nonmonotheists there was
none. In the early sixteenth century, the king of Spain sponsored
a debate at his court to determine whether or not Native Americans had souls; that is, were they human or animal? It was
decided that they were human and, therefore, the Inquisition
applied to them. They could convert or die. Once converted, as
Christians, they could not be enslaved. That part of the Spanish
court's decision was simply ignored by the conquistadors in the
New World.

Polytheists came to be understood by European Christians,
virtually by definition, as either "Noble Savages," promoted by

some French Jesuits in the Americas, or vermin to be eradicated if Native American or enslaved if African. The latter viewpoint was preferred in the British colonies, where Christian missionizing was long forbidden to prevent, in effect, the assumed humanization of non-Caucasians, which would, in turn, necessitate humane treatment.

Thus, those who looked positively on non-Western traditions found them to be protomonotheistic. Those who looked on the very same cultures negatively found them to be polytheistic. Accordingly, many studies of Native American religions assume that above all concepts of the numinous there is a belief in an overriding single Great Spirit, a being who, of course, is male and dominating, in spite of many of the cultures being matrifocal and egalitarian. The Jesuit missionaries in China, from the late sixteenth century, insisted that the Chinese worshipped the Master of Heaven in spite of articulate Chinese denials. Those missionaries in Africa who did not detest Africans, as well as African Christians, assumed for sub-Saharan African religions an overriding male master deity so numinous that he was otiose, that is, ignored in any and all rituals. To my way of thinking, the understanding of a deity as being otiose is simply an admission of cultural imposition.

From my experiences in a number of different cultures, I simply do not understand how a culture can have a deity that is not found in functional myths nor is a recipient of ritual attention. It is a strange deity indeed that is ignored by the humans for whom that entity is supposed to be a deity, especially a deity that fits the Western notions of sex/gender, and absolutism rather than the culture under discussion and, most particularly, a deity that is supreme over all others. In other words, how can a culture that is polytheistic in all regards, to be discussed below, essentially be monotheistic in just this one concept?

In effect, such theories deny that there is any living polytheistic tradition. Teutonic deities can be safely appreciated as indicative of racial qualities additional to the virtues of Christianity for people like Wagner, Hitler, and their ilk, or as comic book action heroes in American culture. Hellenic and Roman polytheistic deities can be dealt with in modern Western schools as the subject of desacralized stories because they are understood to be safely in the distant past and irrelevant to real religion. It is not that we do not have access to the understanding of these deities in their own time and how they were reverenced. The well-known *Metamorphoses* (*The Golden Ass*) by the second-century Apuleius provides a contemporaneous confessional attitude toward and appreciation of Hellenistic deities. The novel includes a critique of monotheism and was probably intended to be a counter to Christianity. From the preceding century of Roman culture, we have the early philosophy of religion text by Cicero, *The Nature of the Gods*, which summarizes the Epicurean and Stoic arguments concerning the deities, as well as counterarguments.

My analyses on this topic are based on a principle of internal cultural logic. This principle assumes that concepts that are irrelevant or contradictory to religious practices, that are illogical to the logical relationship of all other concepts, and that violate the logical integrity of the religion as a whole cannot be an original part of the traditions, let alone foundational. Therefore, such concepts are either not present, imagined by external analysts, or additive. In particular, two concepts frequently cited as present in polytheistic cultures by monotheists, whether consciously or unconsciously, would violate internal logic. First is that of a male creator in cultures which parallel cosmic creation with human biology. A male creator is not only unnatural—it reminds me of male obstetricians attempting to steal birthing from females—but invariably contradictory to the nonmonotheistic religions. The second is that of a single master deity in cultures which are egalitarian and have no notion of a "master," "king," and so on, or in cultures in which the rulers are a married couple. None of these cultures reached the extreme form of patriarchy exemplified by modern Western culture.

One way to avoid the effects of one's ethnocentrism on one's analyses of culture and religion is to oneself internalize the internal logic of the subject culture. The only means to do this of which I am a~~~ ' is first to learn the language to the extent that one categories, which will never, of course, be the same as ɔ's first language. Second, one needs to fully participligious rituals, that is, participate with the mindset ials are utterly meaningful. If one can do this without losing one's original cultural ways of thinking, then one has two or more paradigm systems. To avoid confusion, one then must learn to be self-aware of these paradigm systems and learn to shift between them as appropriate. The comparative enterprise then becomes the comparing of these paradigm systems.

Åke Hultkrantz—the European scholar whom I consider my mentor in the history of religions, and who has published more on Native American religions than any other scholar—and I have long ago agreed to disagree on this topic. For example, he has found a number of very early European reports on the Native American Great Spirit that he considers supportive of an aboriginal understanding because of their similarity and antiquity. To me, this same evidence supports my view of ethnocentrism as the basis of precontemporary ethnology. Of the above mentioned examples of ethnocentric assumptions of the continuing effects of the ur-monotheism concept, two will be presented in greater detail to provide examples of the processes involved.

The Native American "Great Spirit"

Ubiquitous in precontemporary studies of Native North American religions, as well as in the discourses on Native religion by Natives not brought up in the traditions, is a focus on the "Great Spirit." This single deity is often posited as either the real sole deity of Native Americans or a master deity to whom all other deities are subsidiary, the latter being similar to angels in the Religions of the Book. Although the term is not mentioned in seventeenth-century reports, there are confused references to it in eighteenth-century writings, and by the nineteenth century it had become firmly entrenched. In different language and cultural areas, the term seems to have arisen somewhat differently.

Among writings on Algonkian language cultures, a term is presented as the native name for God: Kichi Manitou, "Great Spirit." The term was also used as a translation for "God" among Christian missionaries. According to an Anishnabe (Ojibwa/Odawa) scholar and healer, Kenn Pitawanakwat, the term may have arisen as a confusion over two prefixes: *ke-sha*, meaning "benevolent", and *ki-tchi*, meaning "great," in the sense of "huge" (the pronunciation varying according to dialects). An

Anishnabe speaking of the *manido*, the deities, as benevolent may have been misheard by a European listener as referring to the name of an immense deity, which was understood in the sense of "superior" rather than "huge." *Ki-tchimanido* does not mean "Great Spirit," as is the usual translation; it means "Gigantic Spirit." The same prefix is used in the Algonkian word for Lake Superior; it means "Huge Lake." On the other hand, John Long, a late eighteenth-century English trader, in his writings, implies that the term was a French Jesuit invention. (See Further Readings for reference to further and bibliographic data in these regards.)

Among Iroquoian-speaking people, the concept seems to have developed with the late eighteenth-century revision of Six Nations' religion and society by Geneodiyo, "Handsome Lake," under Quaker tutelage. These revisions included a shift of residential patterns from matrilineal, matrilocal, large, clan dwellings to small, patrilocal, nuclear-family cabins, of female gardening to male farming, of complementary gender leadership to patriarchy, to the persecution and execution of female elders (clan mothers) as witches, and to a religious focus on a Great Spirit. One ethnologist, Elizabeth Tooker, has suggested that the latter concept came about through the conversion of Sky into the Great Spirit or Controller, with the consequent subordination of Earth, and this seems to be the case on listening to the long thanksgiving prayer of the Longhouse tradition, the religious complex that followed from Geneodiyo's cultural revisions and continues to this day.

Among Siouan-speaking cultures, one individual, the Catholic catechist and traditional ritual leader, Nicholas Black Elk, due to the presentation of his thought by two Euroamericans, John G. Niehardt (*Black Elk Speaks*) and Joseph Epes Brown (*The Sacred Pipe*), came to be understood by Euro-Americans as the archetypal traditionalist Native American theologian, somehow representing all the different Native American religions. As his nephew Fools Crow, also a Catholic and a traditionalist religious leader and healer, relates, Black Elk deliberately sought to meld Catholic theology to Lakota rituals in order to save them. In the information Black Elk imparted to Brown, Wakan Tanka, the "Great Spirit," is a virtual monotheistic male god. Among my earliest publications, I argued that this Lakota term without its Christian reading means the deities as a collective entity. The process of transforming a generic term into a singular one can be traced in recorded discussions of three generations of Lakota prior to Black Elk's theological reformulation, from those religious leaders raised prior to the reservations, to those grudgingly adapting to the then new religiocultural impositions, to those converted to Christianity working for missionaries or the American army as translators.

In summary, a close analysis of the quasi- to fully monotheistic Great Spirit in different cultures indicates parallel processes at work. Either through voluntary adaptation or forced conversion, the English language term "Great Spirit" was associated with indigenous concepts or terms that meant something quite different. Nonetheless, the Great Spirit has been a Native religious concept in a number of traditions for a century or more, but it seems not to be originally indigenous.

The "Master of Heaven"

The earliest Christian missionaries in China, if we discount Nestorian Christianity that was present in China twelve hundred years ago, were Jesuits who were admitted to China beyond Macau in the late sixteenth century. Their missionary enterprise in China was exceptional as they admired Chinese culture and promulgated a romanticized version of it in Europe as the model for an enlightened government and culture. It was also extraordinary as they sought government positions, which meant that they took part in state religious rituals. Their gross skewing of Chinese religion to avoid the fact that they were engaged in heretical activities during the time of the Inquisition is another story.

The first Jesuit to enter China, Matteo Ricci, reinterpreted rather, deliberately misinterpreted, the imperial sa~ ''
to Sky and Earth as worship of th~
(*Tianzhu*), a quasi-monotheistic male dei\
the translation for "God" as early as 158
Jesuit theological invention the "King o
Heaven" in Chinese), using more bibl\

claimed that the Chinese were and had always been monotheists, if one excluded what he understood as the later perverse
worship of Satan, by which he meant all of the other Chinese
deities, as well as the ancestral spirits. His utterly misleading
presentation of Chinese religion has remained Western academic
dogma to this day. His terminology parallels the contemporaneous Jesuit creation of the "Master of Life" in regard to Native
American religion. But a Jesuit writing at that time about Native
American religions specifically stated that they did not worship
a Master of Heaven and Earth.

The Chinese objected to this misrepresentation, as it was
logically impossible for there to be a "Master" of Heaven and
Earth, the primary, ever self-creating, equal pair of entities following the ongoing self-creation of the singular Dao from ultimate nonbeing and its splitting into the two generative cosmic
powers, paralleled by the two complementary sources of energy,
yin and yang. The Chinese also noted the Jesuit exclusion of
Earth from the cosmic couple and that the Jesuits objected to
their sacrificing to female spirits, including Earth. Ricci dismissed the Chinese objections with the typical arrogant Western
ethnocentric response: What did the Chinese know about their
own religion, anyway?

Theological Effects of Western Colonialism on Non-Western Traditions

When I have delivered earlier aspects of this treatise, as non-
confessional comparative theology, at meetings of religious
studies societies, invariably someone of Hindu background has
challenged any mention of India, insisting that Hinduism is not
polytheistic. Indeed, often these Western-educated intellectuals
are insulted by the suggestion. British culture impressed on the
Western educated Indian elite that polytheism was not simply
indicative of ignorant superstition, but the mark of an inferior
race, of mindless, subhuman primitivism, which justified British
rule. Various movements developed, such as the Arya Samaj
d the Brahmo Samaj, which expanded a Hindu philosophical
ept of monism, arising from ecstatic religious experience,
theological framework, a framework divorced from all of

the many normative practices of Hindu religion. None of those who have criticized me in this regard carried out the typical Hindu religious practices, and no one I have encountered who daily performs *puja* (ritual offerings) argues that Hinduism is monotheistic. (Max Müller's term "henotheism," relevant to this discussion, will be discussed in the next chapter.)

In sub-Saharan Africa, as mentioned in earlier chapters, given Islamic and Christian monotheistic values which now dominate these cultures due to past imperialism and slave raiding, to term African religions polytheistic is considered pejorative by those who have positive attitudes toward Africans and African culture. Let us take a single example. The Yoruba spirit realm is highly complex and difficult to encapsulate, and it varies in detail between subcultures. All but one of the divinities of Yoruba religion, of central West Africa, are termed *orisa* and were humans who became divinized, as discussed in chapter 5, or are cosmic or nature spirits, discussed in chapter 3. A second group of numinous beings are the ancestors of the family, of major importance for the welfare of families and clans, and deified clan founders and other important clan personages, as discussed in chapter 4. A third category is exceptional and applies but to a single divinity, Olorun, the center of a scholarly debate.

Contemporary Yoruban creation myths begin with Olodumare or Olorun ("owner of sky"), who is genderless, whose abode is in the sky, and who decides to create Earth by converting a marshy plain to solid ground. In one version, It sends Obatala (King of the White Cloth), the chief male deity, to scatter some soil to create the ground. Obatala falls in with a group of divinities drinking palm wine, gets drunk, and falls asleep. Oduduwa, the chief female deity, aware of Obatala's mission, picks up the soil given him by Olodumare and creates the world. In another major version, Olodumare sends the primary deputy, Orisanla ("Great Divinity," who is the same as Oduduwa), to create the world. She comes down from the sky and tosses soil on the water and then turns loose a five-toed hen to scatter the soil about, creating the world on which we live. Subsequently, She creates the Yoruba people. In either case, it is a female deity that creates the world (save for those few written accounts which present both versions of the divinity as male)

Some scholars understand Olodumare to be a late addition to
the cosmogonic myth, perhaps paralleling the shift from a
female to a male king, which another myth strongly suggests.
Regardless of the version, it is a female deity, superior to all the
male divinities (Olodumare is literally above the divinities and
is not understood to be an *orisa*—deity), who creates the Earth,
as is the case with most, if not all, West African traditions. Since
Olodumare is unnecessary to these myths, indeed, complicates
the narrative, it is not unreasonable to assume that the high god,
who is not a deity (*orisa*) in the accepted sense, is a later addition. I will illustrate this process and its ramifications in more
detail with Native American and East Asian examples.

The "Creator"

Modern Native North American religious rhetoric rarely
uses the term discussed above, the Great Spirit, although the
term remains in use among a number of non-Natives presenting
Native religion. Rather, the common term for a single deity is
the "Creator." This is most interesting given that these traditions
tend not to have creation myths and the protagonist of the recreation or emergence myths is invariably named, being one of
the traditional culture heroes (see chapter 6), and is not called
the "Creator." During rituals, English language explanations
will often refer to the Creator, yet the ritual utterances themselves have no reference to a Creator, unless the Sky deity is
called the Creator as the recipient of one of the six ubiquitous
offerings to Sky, Earth, and the Four Directions (see chapter 2).
Prayers offered in Algonkian languages tend to be addressed to
Mishomis (Grandfather), although the connected offerings are to
both Mishomis and Nokomis (Grandmother). In English language versions of these extemporaneous prayers, they are
directed to "Father."

Almost all of these people, middle-aged and older, were
forcibly ʰ⁻¹   to missionary-run boarding schools, where they
                 ı, under pain of severe beatings and other modes
                 ·ture, to speak their language, wear traditional
                 ıair styles, and so on. They were thoroughly
                 simplistic version of Christianity which focused

on Genesis and the Lord's Prayer. God, of course, was presented as singular and male, whose foremost accomplishment was the creation of the world and humans, the latter created for but one end, to worship God who created them.

When I first became involved with Native religious ceremonies, I immediately noted the disparity between the rhetoric and the rituals, as well as the myths. The first major article I wrote on Native American religion, discussed in chapter 1, focused on this disjunction. At the end of the article, when it was not I that was consciously writing, there was an admonition about prayer language neglecting the Grandmothers—utterly politically incorrect, of course, as I, a non-Native, was making suggestions about spirituality to Natives. That admonition was based on the assumption, and subsequent inspiration, that the excision of the female aspect was due to Christian influence.

Soon after the article was published in a Native studies journal, (see Further Readings) I was present at a meeting of Canadian Native elders in central British Columbia. A local male elder was asked to offer opening prayers. But he appeared not alone, as invited, but with his wife, and together they offered prayer addressed to the Grandmothers and Grandfathers. Their people were among the last to come under missionary control. I felt that my assumption had been verified. A dozen years after I wrote the article, I began to hear prayers in Algonkian languages addressed to both Mishomis and Nokomis.

Taiping Religion and the Unification Church

Rather than having their indigenous religious traditions affected by Christian patriarchal monotheism as happened with the traditions of Native North America, in East Asia the opposite occurred—indigenous versions of Christianity developed (which also occurred within Native American cultures to less effect). In the mid-nineteenth century, the Taiping religiopolitical movement conquered nearly all of China. If the European and American governments had not militarily supported the collapsing, foreign Manchu regime, the Taipings might possibly have instituted a strong new dynasty. In the late twentieth century, the Korean Unification Church has become a presence in North American and Europe, in spite of serious antagonism and limited persecution from the dominant powers.

In the mid-nineteenth century, one of the many educated young men, Hong Xiuquan, having failed the civil service examinations with their less than 10-percent pass rate, became sick and during the illness had a vision. Years later he came into contact with an early Protestant missionary tract written in Chinese, the missionaries being present in China as a condition of the peace treaties following the successful aggression of European nations and the United States to push opium in China. From this tract, he was able to interpret his earlier vision. In this vision, he was the younger brother of Christ, and he had traveled to heaven to visit his family, including God the Father, the Mother, as well as Christ and His wife. A congregation formed around him, and the Holy Spirit and God, respectively, possessed two individuals and testified to Hong's identity.

This new religious movement eventually took the name from the sacred text of a religiopolitical movement nearly two millennia in the past and called itself the Great Peace (Taiping) movement. Their goal was to establish the Kingdom of God, the New Jerusalem, on earth by overthrowing the by then corrupt and incompetent foreign Manchu regime. They took over much of central China, establishing a capital at the former early Ming dynasty (the previous native regime) capital, Nanjing, established Hong and his wife as the imperial couple, and made their translation of the Bible the basis of their civil service examination system.

To the foreign Christian missionaries, the idea of a Chinese messiah was anathema, and foreign governments did not want to see a reestablished strong Chinese government. Foreign troops strengthened the Manchu armies, which were commanded by a British general. The Taiping movement was crushed, and in the cataclysm, much of China was destroyed. The resulting hatred of Christian missionaries yet continues in China. One of the first acts of the popularly supported Chinese Communist Party in overthrowing the Nationalist Party, led by nominal Christian Chinese and supported by both the Christian West and the former Soviet Union, was to throw out most Christian missionaries. This action was parallel to that of the Kangxi emperor, who in the eighteenth century threw the missionaries out of China when the Pope sided against the Jesuits in the Rites Controversy, the Kangxi emperor having sided with the Jesuits.

In mid-twentieth-century Korea, following the turmoil of the Japanese occupation and the Western dominated civil war between the northern and southern parts, which tore many families apart, a young man, Moon Sun-myung, had a series of visions about the nature of Christian messianism. In essence, he understood that Jesus was a failed messiah because he was executed before he could marry. God's plan was for humans to live in perfect marriage as the basis of a perfect family. Eve destroyed this plan through her sin, having sexual relations with Lucifer, who took the form of a serpent (remember the "were-snake myths" mentioned in chapter 6). This sin was transmitted to humans ever since through the act of sexual intercourse. The Messiah would redeem humans through a perfect marriage, thereby bringing God's plan to completion.

Moon founded the Unification Church, which understands itself to be fully Christian, and the Church understands Moon and his present wife to have formed a perfect marriage. All those matched and married by Moon and his wife, the Holy Mother, as the True Parents (the true Messiah) form perfect marriages, and their children are accordingly sinless. The Unification Church has been rather successful in Japan, and, although it has but a limited membership in the United States and Europe, it has achieved a notoriety far beyond its numbers. In part, this is because the Unification Church has been financially successful and has appealed mainly to middle-class Jewish and Christian youth.

As with the Taiping of the preceding century, the Unification Church was anathema to Christians: that the Messiah had come again as a Korean was abhorrent. The World Council of Churches has repeatedly turned down the Unification Church's application for membership. Moon was jailed in the United States for tax practices involving a trifling sum claimed to be owed to the government, a claim actually dropped after Moon had been incarcerated. Besides, Moon, weak in English, would never have seen the tax forms except to sign them.

What these two modes of East Asian Christianity have in common, among many features, is an understanding of divinity not as a single entity but as family, that is, multiple. For the Taipings, God was not a single individual but a divine family, and the Holy Spirit and God were separate divinities. For the Unification Church, God and the Savior are not one, and the Messiah is only such as a married couple. Jesus, being a bachelor, never became the Messiah. In other words, monotheism in a polytheistic milieu, one which put family first and foremost, was reinterpreted as a form of polytheism, in which all the deities are unified in a single extended family.

Contemporary Versions of Monotheistic Assumptions

It is very difficult for those enculturated in monotheistic traditions to understand polytheism. It is now generally accepted that there were nonmale deities in early human cultures. But the imposition of a monotheistic mindset tends to create a false understanding. Let me give but a single example that is reflected in much of New Age religion and contemporary Feminist Goddess Worship.

It is quite clear that a female anthropomorphic fertility deity was extremely important in central Anatolia. Female figurines were found in many of the homes thus far excavated at Çatalhöyük, previously mentioned, the oldest permanent, large-scale horticultural settlement so far found, dating to approximately nine thousand years ago. At the Museum of Anatolian Civilization in Ankara, the culture is described as matriarchal, at least in the English language explanation found on the wall. This assumption follows the logic that the female deity was the sole deity, and accordingly, as with the Religions of the Book having a sole male deity and being patriarchal, the culture must have been female dominated. Female fertility deities remained important throughout the history of Anatolia and the rest of present-day Turkey. The considerable importance of the temple to Artemis (Cybele) at Ephesus, on the Aegean coast, remains unquestioned. And it is very possible that the legend of the Virgin Mary moving to Ephesus after the Crucifixion is due to the city being the center of Artemis worship. Two famous,

larger-than-life-sized images of Artemis can be found at the
Ephesus Museum, and the relatively modern statue of Mary at
her supposed house there is obviously modeled on the posture
of the Artemis statues.

But also found at Ephesus are many priapic statues, including the Egyptian deity Bes, who has a long history in Anatolia
and the western Aegean, and Priapus. Throughout earlier
Bronze Age sites, there are many images of a bull deity. Now in
the homes at Çatalhöyük there were many life-sized replicas of
bulls' heads on the walls of the homes, with the female images
having been on platforms or tables (along the same wall?).
Given the continuity of the female fertility deity, how else can
the bulls be understood than as a male deity, in conjunction
with the female deity, especially since both are required for fertility? There are also painted scenes of males hunting, and mace
heads were found, a clear indication of male warrior activities.
Obviously the culture was polytheistic, not monotheistic, and
there is absolutely no evidence for matriarchy, any more than
there is for patriarchy (nor, clearly, was it a peace-loving female
culture with no male influence, as is understood in the Feminist
Goddess Worship myth). The female anthropomorphic figures
most likely represented Earth, who in many cultures, is considered at one with human females, while the bull probably represented Sky, most usually considered male, as discussed in
chapter 3. The museum catalogue, providing more scholarly
interpretations, does not repeat the matriarchal assertion of the
museum display.

Similarly, the argument that there were only female images
of deity in paleolithic cultures only works if one deliberately
ignores all other sacred symbols. In Native American traditions
of the Plains, Earth may be represented by a female anthropomorphic figure or a female bison, while Sky is represented by
the symbol for lightening. In polytheistic traditions, deities of
different genders may be represented by what, to the monotheistic mind, may not be perceived as interrelated images.

No living matriarchal traditions has been found by ethnologists, although there are a number of matrifocal ones. I have
elsewhere argued that matrifocal cultures are superior to patrifocal ones, because patrifocal cultures can proceed to patriarchy

but matrifocal cultures remain egalitarian. Yet based on the above, modern Feminist Goddess Worship posits a peace-loving matriarchal society in the distant past whose religion was monotheistic, the deity being female. This culture was destroyed by an invasion of male warriors who replaced matriarchy with patriarchy and the female monotheistic deity with a male monotheistic deity. But the spiritual problem for women may be monotheism itself (see next chapter), which will not be solved by worshipping a singular Goddess, even if in three (maiden, mother, crone) or hundreds of aspects appropriated from a variety of polytheistic traditions subsumed within a (perhaps unconscious) monotheistic framework. All of those cultures in which women have major religious roles and in which women are empowered by female deities are polytheistic. Bringing into this an understanding of a single deity derived from polytheistic ones may not be as empowering as polytheism itself.

Many other examples can be given of interpreting one deity of a culture as the sole deity, simply because those of Western traditions fail to understand polytheism. Perhaps this book can serve as a corrective.

CHAPTER EIGHT

DIVERSITY AND ACCOMMODATION: HUMAN LIFE IN A POLYTHEISTIC MILIEU

———————❖———————

> *When [Isis] had reached the close of her sacred prophecy, that invincible deity retired to keep her own company. Without delay I was at once released from firm sleep. With mingled emotions of fear and joy I arose, bathed in sweat, utterly bemused by so vivid an epiphany of the powerful goddess. . . . At that moment the clouds of dark night were dispersed, and a golden sun arose. . . . My personal sense of well-being seemed to be compounded by a general atmosphere of joy, which was so pervasive that I sensed that every kind of domestic beast, and entire households, and the very weather seemed to present a smiling face to the world.*
> —Apuleius, *The Golden Ass* (P. G. Walsh translation)

The One in the Many, The Many in the One

Although the previous chapter dismissed as ethnocentric misunderstandings or as influence from monotheistic religions the positing of a single, overarching superior deity, usually

121

male, in polytheistic traditions, polytheism in and of itself does not preclude monistic understandings. Both unitary and multiple understandings of the numinous can be found side by side, either separately or in a complementary fashion in a number of religious traditions. This development can occur in a number of differing ways, including the following: 1) the mystic experience (the experience of utter unity or nothingness) may be related to theological understandings or spiritual practices; 2) devotion to a single deity out of the many available may lead to a conflation of all deities with the deity who is the focus of worship (henotheism); and 3) there may be an understanding of an underlying functional equivalence among all the deities, either as deities or as a source of shamanistic power.

As discussed previously, polytheism does not preclude the understanding of absolute unity or nothingness arising from the mystic experience. A substantial number of persons in any given culture seem to have various types of unitive experiences, experiences of varying degrees of ecstatic states in which one merges with the totality of everything or the divine. And it is far from unusual to become lost in music, art, a beautiful scene, or a sunset, all imparting a feeling of the oneness of everything, without disturbing one's theological understanding, whether monotheistic or polytheistic. A smaller number of individuals have the experience of the self becoming utterly dissolved in the entirety of things, usually experienced as a brilliant, colorless light, or in absolute nothingness—termed the "mystic experience" in this work. With either interpretation, the latter experience is also one of unity, even if that unity is with a nullity. In the polytheistic traditions, this experience of unity or oneness is generally not understood to contradict or deny a polytheistic understanding.

A contradiction is not implicit, because the mystic experience, for example, stands outside of normal functioning, as well as the understandings inherent to culturally determined activities. Indeed, functioning is virtually impossible during the experience, save for routinized dance steps and so on. Knut Rasmussen received from an Inuit (Eskimo) shaman in the early twentieth century a description of the mystic experience that was understood to be the source of his shamanic power. But the experience for the Inuit was not a shamanistic one, for he did not function as a shaman during that experience. When he did so, it was with the assistance of numinous entities; that is, in spite of the experience of utter unity, he functioned from a polytheistic perspective. An Anishnabe (Ojibwe) shaman told me of her own and her mentor's mystic experiences. These experiences were important to him at a time when the Catholic missionary who controlled the reservation on the north shore of Lake Superior did not allow the members of the community to approach him for healing and other related activities. Unable to function shamanistically, he focused on unitive and null ecstatic experiences. These persons functioned with spirits in an ecstatic state when shamanizing and were not then experiencing unity. Similarly, a highly experienced Chinese spirit-possession medium also told me of her mystic experience, which she understood to be separate from the polytheistic theological underpinnings of her religious role.

Within the Hindu traditions, the most common form of spiritual practice is *bhakti*—utter devotion to a single deity (the ubiquitous mode of ritual practice being *puja*, offerings to a deity or other manifestation of the sacred). The tradition understands that it is the practice of devotion in and of itself that is essential; accordingly, the particular deity chosen as the object of devotion is relatively unimportant. Aware of the many Hindu deities, the devotee tends to associate all the attributes of the various deities with the single deity who is the object of devotion. This is not an exclusive relationship; the devotee will make offerings to other deities when in their presence in temples and shrines. But for the devotee, in essence, there is but a single deity. Hindus may also comprehend that in spite of the multitude of deities present in the various Hindu traditions, there is an essential commonality to them in that they are all deities. Moreover, in the Hindu tradition, major deities have avatars—different deities as aspects of the same deity—as well as consorts, who have both similar and different attributes. These are among the many ways that Hindus can be comfortable with monotheistic rhetoric, although for them that rhetoric has a different hermeneutic than for those of the monotheistic traditions, leading to much misunderstanding.

Similarly, all traditions have one or more terms for deities, and the existence of a single term for the deities in and of itself determines a kind of unity and sameness among the deities. In Algonkian languages, the word *manido,* in its various dialectical forms, refers to the deities both singularly and as a generic concept, to anything with a sacred nature, to anything in its sacred aspect, and to sacred or divine power in and of itself (except in some Plains Cree communities, where under Catholic influence, the word has come to refer to a relatively singular male deity). Similarly, in Chinese, the word *shen* may refer to all spirits of any sort. Such words allow speaking of the divine generically in the singular, although it is understood that there are many deities.

In a related linguistic practice, a word may be created for speaking of a group of spirits as a whole. Previously, the Chinese term *shangdi* was introduced. This term was used to refer to a major aspect of the numinous from an undetermined date until about three thousand years ago. As discussed, Protestant missionaries borrowed the term to refer to God, which subsequently was read back into the distant past, leading to the assumption that the early Chinese were monotheists on the Protestant model. But more recent research indicates that the term refers to the dead of the clan, who are powerful spirits, as a collective. Hence, sacrifices to the clan dead were offered to individual spirits as well as all of the spirits of the clan dead collectively.

Analogously, the Siouan-speaking Lakota have the term *wakan,* which refers to the sacred in any aspect or manifestation, as well as a term for the collective of all beings and things that are *wakan* (sacred): *wakan tanka.* After missionaries came to control the Lakota reservations in the late eighteenth century, the term *wakan tanka* was used for God. Subsequently, Lakota traditional ritual leaders who were also Catholic catechists used the term to refer to a male deity who was supreme over the other deities.

In the Athapaskan-speaking Diné cultures of northwestern North America, the word for the numinous simply translates to "Power." This is also the case for at least some of the Dené of the American southwest, such as the Chiricahua Apache. Individuals within the traditions have their own specific relationship with particular attributes of Power, gained through visions, but the terminological reference focuses on the effective attributes of the numinous, rather than names for specific spirits.

Hence, even in a polytheistic theological context, concepts of unity and singularity have their place. My own means of dealing with seeming contradictions in my own spiritual life is to function with multiple paradigms. This is possible because I have actually integrated my thinking with diverse cultures—an unusual mindset, as most humans do not live in a multiplicity of cultures. Accordingly, I interpret my ecstatic experiences of unity, as well as of nothingness, from a Buddho-Daoist perspective, while I help others, when operating in a trance state, from a functional, polytheistic perspective learned from Native traditions. I am still in the process, however, of coming to terms with internally understanding the Chinese perspective on anthropomorphic deities coming to one's assistance via spirit mediums, as well as the related experiencing of beneficial influences coming from my wife's family dead.

A Polytheistic View of Monotheism

As pointed out in chapters 1 and 7, polytheism as a concept makes sense only in a monotheistic world view, for the term means that it refers only to nonmonotheism. Hence, a discussion of polytheism must be presented in its relationship to monotheism. But in this chapter, unlike the preceding one, the discussion will be from the standpoint of polytheism. Whereas the monotheistic traditions have invariably disparaged polytheistic ones, as a polytheist, I perceive the values in reverse. From a polytheistic perspective, monotheistic cultures are comparatively limited and uniform. A tradition with a single deity tends towards cultural acknowledgment of a single truth, a single path, a single end, limited approved personal traits, sometimes a single approved race (Islam excepted) , and, having a number of major ramifications, a single esteemed sex and gender.

Western readers should understand that such an analysis will strain their tolerance, for it will challenge the most basic of their values. The reader should also understand that this analysis is not simply a matter of theoretical speculation, for people from polytheistic cultures have actually experienced their own selves and culture frequently assailed and belittled by those from Western monotheistic traditions. To take as a single example, my wife, who is Chinese, has experienced a half-century of her Chinese religious understanding being attacked by Christian missionaries, American politicians, and even ordinary Westerners as essentially wrong. And she is well aware that this has been going on for over five centuries. She feels most passionately that not only are her Chinese values proper and not problematic, but it is monotheism's insistence on a single truth and intolerance of all others that is the problem. So it is suggested that readers who might be offended by a contrary analysis of some of their most precious values skip the next few pages and move on to the following section.

That extreme patriarchy and monotheism are found together is a fact (whether extreme forms of patriarchy are theoretically necessary to monotheism is a different issue). No matrifocal culture ever developed monotheism; there is no record of a monotheistic Goddess theology until the contemporary Feminist Goddess Worship movement, which has arisen in a patriarchal cultural milieu. Some polytheistic cultures are patriarchal but that patriarchy tends to be limited to certain roles, usually that of rulership, which, however, can lead to other modes of patriarchy.

Accordingly, a seeming consequence of monotheism, given its actual history, and of the nontheistic Buddhism for a different but related set of reasons, is misogyny. To put it another way, from a polytheistic perspective, monotheism is essentially perverse, for in their celebrating a single gender—and in the Religions of the Book (until some recent liberal interpretations) God is not androgynous—fully half of humans and the human experience are necessarily disparaged. No polytheistic tradition celebrates celibacy; in Chinese culture, it is scorned, unless temporary for specific purposes. The major Chinese critique of Buddhism was the celibacy of monks and nuns in the context of the denial of family. Traditional Hinduism does extol celibacy in those modes promoting asceticism as a counter to the normative ritual offerings to the deities, but preferably for the aged, following a life of normal sexuality and family responsibilities. Only celibacy allows for the ignoring of a sex. The practice of celibacy often leads to hatred of the body, especially of the female body by male monks, as is evident in texts arising from both nontheistic Buddhist and monotheistic Christian monasticism.

The concept of a single truth tends towards intolerance, for why, logically, would a culture not feel endangered by falsehood, especially one that is counter to the single self-defining characteristic of the culture? Monotheism generally allows for no greys. Ideas are either true or false. Hence, although science develops out of the alchemy of the medieval Christian milieu (derived from Arabic alchemy, which was stimulated by the much earlier Chinese alchemy), science is not understood by the nonscientific monotheistic population. The general Western public mistakenly thinks science presents unalterable truth, as does their religion, rather than theories to be tested and continually discarded to be replaced by new hypotheses, which is the actual scientific method.

Heresy, the denial of accepted truth, is not comprehensible in a polytheistic milieu. Nor is it possible, since polytheistic religions tend to be experiential and are not creedal. Truth is a matter of personal experience and, to varying degrees in different cultures, accordingly varies from person to person. My truth need not be your truth, but this does not in any way challenge nor imperil my truth or your truth. Indeed, the first Christian heresies, labeled Gnosticism, tended toward polytheism. Marcian posited at least two deities. The *Secret Book of John* interprets God's jealousy as evidence of polytheism, for who were these other gods of whom God was jealous? The history of Christianity is a history of institutional centralization and dominance, as well as a history of declared heresies. Excommunication often meant execution once the Church became the state. Christianity quickly went from a persecuted minority—persecuted because it would not acknowledge the Roman civic deities—to a persecuting majority. I am well aware that a couple of centuries ago this very presentation within a Christian civilization would have automatically led to my own torture and execution, as it still would in certain Islamic countries.

Monotheism may further lead to fanaticism. The semi-monotheistic Taiping movement, discussed in chapter 7, led to a state-mandated intolerance hitherto unheard of in Chinese culture. In an earlier time, when Buddhist institutions challenged the state, not necessarily deliberately, with regard to economic control, the state fought back with suppressions, but not persecutions. (The Western language literature on this topic tends to use the term "persecution" inaccurately.) The number of monasteries and the land these monasteries could own, as well as the number of monks and nuns within a monastery, were limited but not outlawed, and there was absolutely no concern with individual religious views and practices.

The state simply did not tolerate institutional challenges to its own supremacy; no government does if it is to survive. This is an attitude toward religious institutions that continues in contemporary China: if an institution is not subject to state control, especially if it challenges the state for supremacy, it is considered seditious.

It appears that only the Religions of the Book have gone to war over religious ideology per se. Other cultures and civilizations certainly have warred, but the reasons tend to be territorial, economic, and so on. It may seem that the case of the Tamil-speaking people in Sri Lanka is an exception, but this conflict seems to be over ethnicity and language, rather than religious ideas. On the other hand, it must be admitted that there is a strain of intolerant Hinduism in contemporary India, and there are instances of related behavior in the past.

To shift to another topic, wedded to the Western sense of linear time, monotheism mandated the notion of a creator. The concept of creation led to a separation of the Creator and the created. Earth and all of nature were desacralized. Humans, being natural beings, thus lost their divine nature. During World War II, Americans greatly misunderstood the character of Japanese religion. They thought that the Japanese worshipped the emperor as divine in the same manner that Christians do God. They required the emperor to renounce his divinity on radio, most difficult for him to do as he would not have thought of himself as such. In actuality, the Japanese understand themselves and all those born on the sacred Japanese islands to have a *kami* (sacred) nature. The emperor simply has more of it, because, as with the Chinese imperial families, his family, as all Japanese aristocratic clans, is descended from a deity. Indeed, the Japanese imperial family is understood to be descended from the most powerful *kami*, Amaterasu, the female Sun deity. Hence, it was not a matter of a qualitative difference between the Emperor and the Japanese people but a quantitative one.

In the polytheistic traditions, the tendency is to understand the world around us not as created but creating. Humans too, as part of the world, are not created, not an object of creation, but both simultaneously creator and created. As the Chinese so long ago put it, humans are self-creating (a continuing creation), as is everything else (*ziran*).

On a connected theme, Christians who had the mystic experience, the experience of nothingness or totality, were more likely to be condemned by the Catholic Church, as was Meister Eckhart, than celebrated, as in India, although this is not true for all of Christianity. The Orthodox tradition, for example, values the mystic experience. For the mystic experience is of the essential sameness of everything, necessarily including deity, and monotheism often finds difficulty in accepting an equivalence between Creator and created, as reiterated, for example, by the early Church Father, Irenaeus. Hence, Christian mystics had to develop theological formulations, such as the concept of the Godhead, that allowed for ecstatic union and disappearance within the understanding of a Creator and a separate creation. Eckhart's nominal heresy was describing God as a "Nothingness," a normative understanding in South Asian and East Asian mystical thinking, although the real heresy was preaching in the vernacular, German, that people could experience God without the intervention of the Church.

Monotheism led to a new understanding of the world; the cosmos became transformed. Instead of all the directions being divine, only a single direction, above, was accorded divinity. The sky (thunder) god was the single divinity, and the sky god's home was the single divine realm. God was in Heaven, and there was no counterbalancing, numinous Earth. Below had become the locus of evil: Hell, the realm of the Devil.

When there is but a single positive direction, as in the monotheistic traditions (save for directing worship toward Jerusalem in Judaism and Mecca in Islam as the sacred centers), so there is but one positive gender. If males, created in the image of God, are good, then the logical corollary is that females are

evil. And so the early Church Fathers, under misogynist inspiration, developed the unique notion of "original sin." Sin was
committed by the first female, and she infected all subsequent
humans with her evilness. Only the male Son of God could
redeem humans from the evilness of the female Eve.

The loss of gender complementariness, the pairing of Sky
and Earth, meant a fundamental change in the nature of dual-
ism; all opposites came to be understood as antagonistic and
absolute: for example, good versus evil (presently understood as
capitalism versus communism, true religion versus godless-
ness). For this reason, the Chinese complementary pair yinyang
is often considerably misunderstood in the West, for none of the
oppositions in the concept includes good versus evil. Polytheistic cultures tend not to have a concept of evil, other than recog-
nizing the human tendency towards selfishness, which, in these
often intrinsically communal societies, was the epitome of antisocial behavior. As mentioned in earlier chapters, among Native
Americans, those in the past who were perceived to function
shamanically for personal advantage were liable to be killed by
their own relatives (to avoid vendettas) for being dangerous to
their own community. In classical Chinese philosophy, the opposite of the public weal, the determinative of the "good" is selfishness, which is understood as natural but undesirable and to
be eradicated through education. The concept of evil is different,
for it requires the separation of humans from the rest of nature;
the ability to choose between good and evil becomes the distin-
guishing characteristic of humans in monotheistic theology.

In polytheistic religions, there tends to be no equivalent of
the relationship between God and the Devil. The deities are usually morally neutral; although some tricksters may be capricious
and a few dangerous, none are evil. For example, in China there
is a concept of dangerous wandering ghosts (those dead who
have no family to care for them or who died under anomalous
circumstances such as suicides). If they possess humans, they
can cause illness or misfortune, and an exorcist is needed to get
rid of them. But, as discussed in chapter 5, sometimes they act
beneficently and become deities. Temples are built for them in
gratitude by those who have been aided by them. In shamanistic
traditions, humans may elicit the aid of these neutral spirits to

help or harm other humans, but it is then the human action which tends toward being approved (good) or disapproved (bad, not evil), with regard to whether the intent of the action is social or antisocial.

Given these differences, how is it that monotheistic traditions have been able, via voluntary or forced conversions, to supplant many polytheistic traditions around the world? Of course, the monotheistic answer would be that the Truth overcomes falseness or wickedness. But this answer would not make sense from a polytheistic perspective.

As mentioned above, the concept of a single truth can lead to a fanatic single-mindedness. Monotheists tend to not give up, and many would and did kill those who refused to convert to "save their souls" (as in Vietnam, where the United States military destroyed a village in order to save it from evil communism). While this attitude would explain a monotheistic tradition successfully dominating contiguous cultures, it would not explain their spread over much of this planet. For example, Buddhism is also a proselytizing tradition, albeit not a ruthless one. It slowly spread into contiguous cultures, not reaching Japan until about fifteen hundred years ago, a thousand years after its founding, and Europe but a couple of centuries ago. Islam spread much faster, and Christianity exploded on the world with the circumnavigation of the planet.

Therein, I think, lies the key. I came to this realization after traveling southward from Anatolia, the earliest known locale of agricultural urbanism, to the Mediterranean coast and boarding a wooden vessel similar to those used in the past. The Mediterranean, being virtually a landlocked sea, although subject to storms, is relatively calm and has no difficult tides. In contrast, for example, the seas between China and Japan are extremely rough. Early seafarers there often did not know within hundreds of kilometers where they would make landfall, if they were fortunate enough to do so. Shipping in China was primarily along the major rivers and the seacoast. Before the Europeans arrived, there was sea travel throughout the Caribbean, a very calm sea outside of the hurricane season. But as there were no large-scale cultures on the islands, as there were on the mainland, there was no major maritime commerce. And Polynesians were the

world's first master mariners, but their long-distance ocean journeys were for small-scale colonization, not large-scale trade.

Given the nature of the Mediterranean and the growth of
distinctive civilizations in different parts of the eastern Mediterranean, it is far from surprising that more than one civilization
arose based on maritime mercantilism, examples being the
Greeks and the Phoenicians, the former speaking an Indo-European language and the latter, a Semitic language. Even earlier,
the Sumerians had been engaged in an active maritime mercantilism with the Indus Valley civilization across the Arabian Sea.

Both Christianity and Islam arose in this environment.
Christianity spread along the coastal port cities of present-day
Turkey and then to Rome and other parts of the Mediterranean.
Later, Islam spread along the caravan routes of central Asia, as
did Buddhism many centuries earlier. But Islam also spread
throughout the southern Mediterranean and over to the
Mediterranean coast of the Iberian peninsula, and around the
Arabian sea over to India and Southeast and East Asia.
Although the Western Roman Empire fell, it was replaced by the
Italian mercantile city-states, the continuation of Byzantium, and
the spread of Islam—it was the maritime, mercantile city of
Roman Catholic Venice that first conquered Eastern Orthodox
Constantinople (present-day Istanbul), not Islam.

The point of the above is that monotheistic single-mindedness was wedded to a constantly expanding maritime mercantilism. Islam had a major sea trade with China from the eleventh
century, and the religion spread throughout the islands and
peninsulas of present-day Indonesia and Malaysia. When Portu-
gal, Spain, Holland, and England sought to break the Islamic
trade monopoly with Asia via the Italian mercantile cities, they
called upon Italian, as well as their own, navigators to explore
new sea routes. Christianity spread militantly with the maritime
merchants. International trade for the early European sea
traders was no different from piracy: foreign towns were pil-
laged and the inhabitants raped and massacred. The Spanish
and Portuguese conquistadores were the same warriors who
drove Jews and Muslims from the Iberian Peninsula. The two
enterprises were understood as one. It was the combination of a
ruthless mercantile greed with a brutal missionary zeal that saw

the spread of Christianity wherever force was ultimately successful. Of course, there were exceptions, including Christian missionaries who devoted their lives primarily to helping others and only secondarily, if at all, to converting them.

If monotheism and polytheism are ideologically in opposition as I assume, then how is one to understand the examples of convergence that have developed? In the case of the African Brazilian and African Carribean situations, the African religions were proscribed in the Americas and continued underground in the guise of Catholic Christianity. The *orixás* were paired with Catholic saints and worshiped in that guise. When Candomblé, for example, was legalized in Brazil, the tradition of convergence had become ingrained. Initiations of mediums take place both in the *terreiro* and the church. But in these examples, it seems that Christianity is perceived as polytheistic, for the focus is on the saints.

After Vatican II, on the north shore of Lake Superior there developed the Jesuit-run Anishnabe Spiritual Centre. Native people who in the past had been forced to become Christians were now encouraged to incorporate traditional practices into church services. At least one Anishnabe Jesuit became a Native healer and functions shamanistically while remaining a Catholic priest. My impression is that for these priests, their religious understanding remains monotheistic with an understanding that the *manido* are on the level of saints under a single deity. In both examples, the practitioners seem to be primarily either montheists or polytheists, not both simultaneously.

Living Polytheism

The above sets out major conceptual and cultural differences between monotheism and polytheism, but it does not enter into the latter's hermeneutics. What does it mean to live with and within a polytheistic worldview? How are polytheistic deities actually experienced and understood? Here, again, I am but aware of and therefore can but discuss my own personal understanding and the understandings gained from my own participation in living Chinese and specific Native North American traditions, as well as informal discussions with ritual leaders and scholars within these and related traditions.

The world I inhabit is a rich one, for it, in and of itself, is sacred. When I walk in nature, everything I encounter is numinous, with some beings more numinous for me than others. I never know when I will have a holy encounter, when a sacred being will be with me, will speak to me. Whenever I see Moon at night, I greet my Grandmother. This is not an intellectual construct. Each time, and the feeling never weakens, I feel a surging of emotion in my breast. I do know the moon is also a huge rock. I will never forget driving eleven hundred miles in thirteen hours across the plains of the northern United States so as not to miss witnessing the televised first landing on the moon, but that is and yet is not the same moon. She is still my Grandmother, and, at my age, the only grandmother I have. Similarly, I greet Sun at sunrise as Grandfather, my grandfather. Needless to say, when I unexpectedly encounter those beings I referred to in chapters 2 and 3—fortunately I am often outside of urban areas and seem to meet them frequently—the feeling of affection is almost overwhelming. Of course, I can bring these entities forth through rituals, but the seemingly chance encounters in nature elicit more of an emotional response, because I did not will them; They did.

This brings us to another aspect of the relationships. That these sacred powers will help me in my work, whether healing or protecting individuals or groups, or doing the same on a larger scale through intellectual endeavors, always leaves me with feelings of awe and immense responsibility. That these deities will act on my request in the service of others or even temporarily merge with me so that I can act directly with their powers does not leave me feeling powerful. Rather, it is the opposite: I am humbled. For it is not me at all; they have all the power. Without them, I can do nothing.

Obviously, from the above, I am most comfortable with a foraging mindset and a shamanistic mode of relationship. In this regard, I am virtually a throwback, an anachronism. Yet this mindset can be but a pale reflection of someone brought up in such a cultural context and whose first language incorporates these understandings. I am uncertain that in the modern world we can imagine what it would be like when everything we ate, every item of clothing or decoration, every aspect of our dwellings came from beings who were asked to give themselves for human use, and when we lived in a community where everyone shared this worldview, where none other was conceivable, and where all of these gifts were allocated in various complex ways among our neighbors. When it comes to other modes of polytheism, my experience is even far more tenuous, as it is more vicarious than direct.

But this is changing. When I was last in Taiwan, as we were driving down a highway, we could not help notice, due to a huge statue visible from the road, a rural monastery with a large temple dedicated to the dipsomaniac deity, Jigong (discussed in chapter 6). Noted especially for His healing powers, Jigong is a highly popular deity, and a favorite of mine. Several of the many visiting the temple that day were possessed by Him and began to heal those who approached. One possession in particular attracted my attention, as well as others: a middle-aged woman who used no props (the usual distinctive costume, wine gourd, and palm-leaf fan). But as Jigong possessed her, her movements were clearly those of an increasingly tipsy person drinking from an invisible vessel held in the hand. As I came near while He was healing the many who crowded around Him, a feeling a joy spread through me; the deity's intoxicated exuberance was contagious. The deity's presence was unmistakable. The glow, the high, stayed with me for the remainder of the day.

Religiocultural contexts in which one's family itself is the primary sacred entity is even more removed from contemporary North American culture than foraging ones. For we modern North Americans are enculturated to value individual independence above all. We prize children having their own private quarters within the family home and expect them to leave the home on finishing secondary school. Increasingly, school and social agencies, often unwittingly, encourage children to become independent at the onset of puberty. In Ontario, where I have spent the last three decades, children who leave home are given money by the municipal governments for shelter and food, regardless of the reasons for leaving, even if the reason is but seeking independence from a modicum of parental control. Parents who seek to bring them back from the life on the streets are liable to be jailed. Life under these circumstances becomes meaningless for many, and children, even before adolescence, begin to experiment with mind-altering chemicals. In a culture of the religion of familism, such behavior would be uncommon, for we would not understand ourselves to be independent beings.

Within the family-religion milieu, the modern American Christian sentiment, "The family that prays together stays together," is incomprehensible. For a family that prays to itself rather than to some distant, different being does not conceive of not staying together, save for reasons considered useful to the family, for example, fleeing famine or war so that the family line can continue or going off to a distant job to enhance the family's fortunes.

I remember being invited out to dinner many decades ago to an exclusive club in Osaka by the chief executive officer of a large Japanese family corporation (whom I happened to meet through *kendo*—see chapter 3). He wondered how I was able to receive permission from my family to travel abroad. In spite of his maturity, wealth, and power, he had no independence from his family. It was inconceivable to him, even though I was then in my mid-twenties, that I had never even thought of seeking such permission. In Chinese and related cultures, when the primary focus of religious ritual is the plaques with the names of the family dead on the altar in the main room of the dwelling, when minor offerings are a daily event and every major meal is a sacrificial offering to the family dead before these name plaques, when every change in status or fortune of each member of the family is ritually announced in front of the name plaques, one feels oneself a small part of a larger being, a being that exists more in time than it does in space.

For those whose family identification is enhanced by clan activities, that conception is even stronger, particularly for the sex of the hereditary line, whether matrilineal or patrilineal. In patrilineal China, clan identification meant that many males involved themselves with rituals in clan temples and had access to books recording a family entity that went back many generations. Those associated with an imperial heritage understood the family to have divine origins. Two thousand years ago, females identified with the natal line as well as that of their husbands, and this identification is returning with the present one-child policy. In these religious traditions, one is not responsible to oneself or even the nuclear family, but to the larger family as a sacred entity. It is no accident that the family name is given precedence over individual names, for the former has far more meaning than the latter. Everything one does is to preserve and, if possible, enhance the family. Every personal failure affects not oneself, but the divine, the sacred family.

There have been many analyses of the differences between shame and guilt cultures, but few seem to comprehend that the difference arises from fundamentally different religious perceptions. This difference is between the concept of sacred family, necessarily polytheistic since the family as a whole is still comprised of many entities, living and dead, and the Religions of the Book, in which one inevitably must disobey some of the many injunctions flowing from a single Lord. In the Orthodox Jewish tradition in which I was raised, the injunctions were not limited to the Ten Commandments but extended to hundreds of rules regarding every aspect of our behavior. Every action was a either a blessing glorifying God or a sin against God. Given our imperfections, especially for a child or youth, guilt was continual and unending. In Catholicism, confession and repentance is expected to be a never-ending process, and those Protestant sects with an understanding of predestination assume that but a small proportion of humanity will avoid the fires of Hell. All are guilty of original sin.

In the sacred-family context, every action augments or diminishes the family. But one does not act alone, for one can call upon the dead spirits of the family for assistance; after all, these spirits are family and feel about the family as one does. While not all powerful, so long as they are not forgotten, one has confidence that they are trying their best to enhance one's fortunes, in turn enhancing that of the family. Hence, one strenuously avoids being shamed, for the shame falls not on oneself but on the family and, particularly, the family dead. In imperial times, a person was rewarded for exceptional service by titles being given posthumously to dead members of his family. This

practice is reflected in the giving of titles by the emperor to powerful deities, who, after all, are but dead nonfamily humans.

This brings us to reflect that the Chinese religious sensibility
is not limited to the family, but includes a host of deities of
many types. When offerings are made at a temple, it is not only
to the primary deity of the temple, if there is one, but to all the
deities present through their images. In the suburbs of Tainan,
the old city in southern Taiwan, a new temple has been built to
house the oldest image of Mazu in Taiwan, brought from Fujian
Province at the beginning of Chinese colonization. The original
temple had become too small to hold the many devotees who
thronged to make offerings. The new temple is huge, with three
successive courtyards of temple complexes, along with courtyards to both sides housing hotels, restaurants, and offices. Outside, there is an enormous parking lot, similar to those
surrounding American sports stadiums.

Those who come do not make offerings only before this
ancient image of Mazu but to every image. I have observed
family after family with bundles of stick incense and candles
going from deity to deity, from temple building to temple building within the enormous complex, making their offerings. This
is the advantage of polytheism: the more the better. One has
nothing to lose by making offerings to every available deity.
Polytheistic deities, in contrast to the monotheistic one, seem not
to be jealous of each other, and they do not punish for being
slighted (extant Hellenic myths, assuming they actually capture
Hellenic mythic understanding, seem to be an exception),
although one cannot expect benefits if one does ignore those
important to one's life. If a particular deity does not help one,
perhaps another will. Indeed, when good fortune comes, one
may be uncertain as to which deity is responsible. So one goes
back to the temple again to make offerings to all the deities present to make sure that one's gratitude reaches the effectual deity,
as well as the temple that houses the deity.

This aspect of polytheism is close to many forms of Christianity, although one could argue, as would a number of Protes-
tants, that these versions are not truly monotheistic. In a Roman
Catholic or Orthodox Church one can similarly watch persons,
more commonly individuals than families, offer candles before

the images of a multiplicity of saints and, similarly, reward the church itself if their prayers are granted. Modern Catholicism tacitly recognizes this correspondence. Vatican II reinstated the Jesuit position in the Rites Controversy that accepted the continuation of ancestral offerings for converted Chinese. Today, one can see in the homes of Chinese Christians in Taiwan shrines with ancestral name tablets before which offerings are made of incense and food. Often included is an image of Mary in place of the traditional Guanyin.

Similarly, contemporary liberal Protestant sects in North America consider themselves in spiritual, rather than theological, harmony with Native religion. I have had the privilege of being in spirit [sweat] lodges in Canada that included both Native traditionalist elders and Anglican and United Church Native ministers. On the other hand, in Victoria where I now reside, I recently experienced Chinese converts to Evangelical Christianity not being allowed by their church to visit the local Chinese temple even in a nonparticipatory way.

In the most common forms of polytheism there are many numinous entities that are specific to the variety of human needs. Deities are not thought of as all powerful, but as having specialities, and we turn to the one or several most suitable to a particular need. These needs may be occupational or of health, broadly understood. Because the deities are not assumed to be omnipotent, deities may not be successful with regard to human requests. Some may lose their power altogether or no longer be interested in aiding humans; they can be identified by their neglected temples. If a request to a deity goes unfulfilled, we simply make the request to another deity. Nonetheless, the deities cannot counter fate but can only enhance what the way of the cosmos permits.

This latter point is poorly understood in the West. Western scholars, permeated by monotheistic assumptions, on the whole, have misunderstood the polytheistic notion of fate. For example, the Chinese concept of *tienming* has been translated as "the Mandate of Heaven," understood as commands from an all-powerful, anthropomorphic, male, quasi-monotheistic deity. The term actually and literally means the "pattern of the sky." As in the premodern West, astrology (not the simplistic Western astrology of today, which has little to do with actual observations) and astronomy were not divorced. In traditional China, astronomy-astrology was the focus of a government office. The Jesuits were brought into this branch of the Chinese government in the seventeenth century, because it was thought that their different astronomical knowledge could enhance astrological computation.

It is assumed that there is a pattern to the flow of the cosmos, but it is one that is dynamic rather than static. In the Chinese understanding, there is but a single constant: change, in and of itself. Hence, the name of the earliest extant Chinese text, a diviner's manual that also became a philosophical text with the attachment of appendices, is simply named *Change* (*Yi*). A major purpose of astronomy was to note changes in the sky, especially those exceptional to the normal pattern, and to attempt to interpret how governmental policy could be modified to accord with the natural flow, so as to be successful or avoid disaster. Even to the present day diviners are utilized for this purpose. Major businesses and corporations in Taiwan, Hong Kong, and Singapore avail themselves of this knowledge to assist in making business decisions.

Thus, the deities, being dead humans, cannot thwart the natural pattern. If their requested assistance fails, no blame is attached to them, and there is no assumption of their willfully not allowing healing or whatever to take place. If, for example, it is our time to die, nothing can change this, for it is not determined by a deity but by the natural pattern, the Way (*dao*). Theodicy, accordingly, is irrelevant within polytheism. To use a contemporary phrase, and please pardon the use of colloquial language, "shit happens." We make requests of the deities for assistance on the chance that what is happening negatively is not fixed or what we wish to happen positively is within the realm of possibilities of the natural pattern. That being the case, the deities, through their intervention and powers, can effect the desired result. But if it is not the case, there is little that they can do. The deities do not need to be appeased, and they certainly do not require praise, save for accomplished deeds of the present.

Finally, the deities are not distant beings. We literally confront them. As in Catholic and Orthodox Christian churches, the images of the numinous embody their sacredness. An offering to the image is an offering to the saint or deity. Images are omnipresent on Chinese multifunctional family altars (but not on clan altars) alongside the family tablets as statuettes and behind as pictures. Every village and urban neighborhood has a temple housing many images, and the local people are frequently in and around the temple as it is the only public space. Travel for nonoccupational purposes often involves pilgrimages to especially sacred locales and their temples. In any case, in traditional China, monasteries housing Daoist or Buddhist temples on their grounds often served as inns for travelers. Similarly, in traditional Native American Pawnee and Mandan lodges, there was an altar with a sacred ear of corn and a bison skull which were fed daily. And, of course, there are many Native American sacred pilgrimage sites, which Native Americans today are attempting through the courts to preserve from exploitation, usually unsuccessfully, or to even gain access. In other words, in polytheistic traditions, the deities are ubiquitous, as other modes of sacred presence are visibly omnipresent in the Religions of the Book, such as in the Torah, Bible, and Qu'ran. The difference is the presence of many deities in and of themselves.

As in Pentecostal Christianity, one can be possessed by the numinous. In this tradition, if possessed by the Holy Spirit, a person can heal with the power of God. Similarly in most polytheistic traditions from Africa through South and East Asia to Oceania, as well as African-influenced traditions in the Americas, deities are experienced directly through their possessing humans, as discussed in chapters 5 and 6. The difference with regard to Pentacostalism is that the possession in polytheistic cultures tends to be total: only the medium's body is present; the medium her- or himself is simply not there. (Possession is often actually total in Pentacostalism but is not acknowledged as such; rather one is understood to have been struck by the power of the Lord.) The deity is fully present in the flesh and voice of the medium in mediumistic traditions. The deity can touch you and you can touch deity; these are highly tangible religions.

In the foraging traditions, of course, the deities are omnipresent. Every breath of air, every drink of water, every bit of light from the sun and moon, the ground on which we tread, every plant and animal we encounter, the material of our shelters, the garments and adornments we wear, every bite of food—all are numinous.

We must experience these cultures to understand what it means to people to encounter their deities directly. We can tell a deity our problems and directly receive the deity's advice or healing. There can be no element of doubt nor the necessity of faith when we know rather than believe we are in the presence of a deity. And this is not a rare happenstance; it occurs frequently, indeed, in some cultures, such as China, on demand. Hence, the deities can be directly experienced as often as we need; they are palpably omnipresent.

Conclusions

All of the above means that polytheism at best is a very positive human experience and is never less than benign. We do not find the angst, let alone the doubts, that many experience with regard to their relationship with the divine in the monotheistic traditions. The deities are not history in and of themselves and do not cause everything that happens. They are there for those who seek them, even sometimes there for those who do not seek them. They can resolve doubts by speaking (or writing) to their devotees. They do not lay down rules for humans to follow, although a particular personal relationship may involve obligations for the human in return for favors from a deity. Rather, the rules of human life arise from family and community concerns, ethical considerations, and the way of the universe. In China, as well, deities tend to reiterate the social importance of moral conduct, particularly in their writing via spirit possession. These rules for living are not imposed by an anthropomorphic deity; moral conduct means that humans can best live by harmonizing their actions with nature, society as a whole, and the inevitable. Thus, if we suffer from disasters, whether natural or caused by other humans, we do not need to blame ourselves for angering some deity or not following some divinely preordained course of action.

This does not, of course, mean that if we fail in to meet a specific obligation we or those close to us may not suffer. Hence, in the Inuit tradition, in times of famine, a shaman would seek out the deity responsible and attempt to discover if anyone violated the customs relating to the sought-after food source. On the other hand, in traditional China, in times of drought, the deity responsible was made to suffer, first by placing the image of the deity out in the hot sun and, if that did not work, exposing the deity within a possessed human to the burning sun. A variety of deities allows for a variety of possibilities.

Polytheistic deities tend to be more companionable than a single, absolute, monarchial deity. Among the terms for the Chinese emperor was "the Single Person" (*yiren*). It is lonely at the top. The emperor could not relax with anyone; the separation of the sexes in this culture meant that the emperor probably could not even fully relax with his consort. Polytheistic deities have no status to maintain. If they help people, it is because they want to, so they are likely to be friendly, depending on their nature—I certainly would not expect nor want to become too cozy with Thunder. But I do enjoy the presence of some deities with whom I would not advise being close without a special relationship. Similarly, in Christianity, people are far more comfortable with Mary than with the Father, or even Jesus.

Perhaps I can summarize with a single sentence. Polytheism is more than useful, it is enjoyable. That is, polytheism has not just made my life more meaningful—literally the opposite of my Buddho-Daoist self—it has made my life exhilarating.

Further Readings

❖

Exceedingly few books are written from a polytheistic perspective, and those unaffected by a monotheistic mindset are rarer still. Hence, further study, aside from direct experience, requires both judicious reading and perusing small germane parts of a large number of works. In the following, a sampling of books is suggested. The list does not include a much larger number of relevant works that require background in the discipline in which the books were written or with regard to the subject cultures, as well as technical journal articles.

Chapter 1

As discussed at the beginning of chapter 1, the topic of polytheistic theology, especially from a comparative perspective remains virtually untouched. Michael York's *Pagan Theology: Pagan Theology as a World Religion* (New York: New York University Press, 2003), represents a recent attempt that, unfortunately, fails to do the subject justice. Yet it remains the only alternative to this study as an example of another approach.

As mentioned in the chapter, Apuleius's *The Golden Ass* provides a highly readable, indeed most enjoyable, view into the mind of a Hellenistic polytheist aware of but not influenced by monotheism. A relatively new translation is available by P. G. Walsh (New York: Oxford University Press, 1994).

Also as mentioned, my evolving understanding of this topic, as well as the influences of the cultures in which I have been a participant observer, can be found in three of my previous books: *Offering Smoke*, *The Spirits Are Drunk*, and *Through the Earth Darkly* (see the preface for full titles and publication details). The bibliographies and bibliographic notes in these books contain numerous references to studies pertinent to the themes covered in this book.

We learn of the deities either from direct experience or the telling of myths, most of which are oral. In our highly literate culture, we have lost not only an appreciation but an understanding of the telling of myths. Robert Bringhurst's *A Story As Sharp As a Knife: The Classical Haida Mythtellers and Their World* (Vancouver: Douglas & McIntyre, 1999) goes far in presenting the complexities of myth in and of itself (as compared to the usual truncated versions in anthologies), as well as the aesthetics and other facets of mythtelling.

Chapter 2

The Chinese understanding is further developed in *The Spirits Are Drunk* (see above) with regard to Sky and Earth and Mountains and Streams. Extracts from relevant texts will be found in Jordan Paper and Lawrence G. Thompson, *The Chinese Way in Religion* (Belmont, CA: Wadsworth, 1998). The Native North American understanding is developed in *Offering Smoke* (see above), concerning Sky, Earth, and the Four Directions. A more comprehensive presentation with regard to a single North American Native culture will be found in James R. Murie, *Ceremonies of the Pawnee* (in 2 parts), ed. by Douglas R. Parks (Washington, D.C.: Smithsonian Contributions to Anthropology no. 27, 1981), particularly with regard to Morning Star / Evening Star. The detailed presentation of the indigenous Andean understanding of Sky will be found in a work by the ethnoastronomer, Gary Urton, *At the Crossroads of the Earth and the Sky: An Andean Cosmology* (Austin: University of Texas Press, 1981), but the focus is primarily of Sky. Hence, the work is best read for balance with a work by the feminist ethnohistorian, Irene Silverblatt, *Moon, Sun, and Witches: Gender Ideologies and Class in Inca and Colonial Peru* (Princeton: Princeton University Press, 1987), for her discussion of Pachamama (Earth Mother) and associated deities. Relevant to this chapter and the following is Daniel Merkur's *Powers Which We Do Not Know: The Gods and Spirits of the Inuit* (Moscow, Idaho: University of Idaho Press, 1991). Based on a thorough reading of the ethnohistorical record, this work presents the Inuit (Eskimo) understanding of both cosmic and animal spirits.

Chapter 3

A comprehensive study of animal spirits in a single culture, aside from *Powers Which We Do Not Know* (see above), is Joseph Epes Brown, *Animals of the Soul: Sacred Animals of the Oglala Sioux* (Rockport, Mass.: Element Press, 1992). Perhaps the sole discourse on the indigenous understanding of plant spirits and the relevant rituals in a horticultural-hunting society will be found in chapter 4, "The Garden's Children," of Michael E. Brown, *Tsewa's Gift: Magic and Meaning in an Amazonian Society* (Washington, D.C.: Smithsonian Institution Press, 1985). The ritual interrelationship of plant and animal spirits, particularly Corn and Bison, in another horticulture-hunting society will be found in *Ceremonies of the Pawnee* (see above). For an inside understanding of shamanism in relation to hunting, see F. Bruce Lamb, *Wizard of the Upper Amazon: The Story of Manuel Córdova-Rios*, 3rd ed. (Berkeley: North Atlantic Books, 1971.) A contemporary Anishanabe expression of the traditional sacred interrelationship between plants and humans will be found in Ken Pitawankwat and Jordan Paper, "Communicating the Intangible: An Anishnabeg Story," *American Indian Quarterly* 20 (1996): 451–65.

Chapter 4

For ancestral spirits and related mediumism with regard to China, see *The Spirits Are Drunk* (above), and David K. Jordan, *Gods, Ghosts, and Ancestors: Folk Religion in a Taiwanese Village* (Berkeley: University of California Press, 1972), lucidly written from an anthropological perspective. A highly readable, sociological perspective on the role of ancestral spirits in daily life is Francis L. K. Hsu's *Under the Ancestors' Shadow: Kinship, Personality and Social Mobility in China* (Stanford: Stanford University Press, 1967). With regard to Central East African understandings of ancestral spirits, see Jacob K. Olupona, *Kingship, Religion, and Rituals in a Nigerian Community* (Stockholm Studies in Comparative Religion No. 28, Stockholm: Amlqvist & Wiksell, 1991). For Polynesian traditions specific to Hawaii see Mary Kawena Pukui, E. W. Haertig, and Catherine A. Lee, *Nānā I Ke kuma (Look to the Source)*, vol. 1 (Honolulu: Queen Lili'uokalani Children's Center Publications, 1972); readers may wish to ignore the psychiatric reductionism added by the non-Hawaiian authors.

Chapter 5

For African deities and related mediumism, see *Kingship, Rituals, and Religion in a Nigerian Community* (above). For the related African Brazilian religion, see Serge Bramly, *Macumba: The Teachings of Maria-Jose, Mother of the Gods* (London: St. Martin's Press, 1977), and a novel by a Candomblé adherent, Jorge Amado's delightful and hilarious *Shepherds of the Night*, translated by Harriet de Onís (New York: Alfred A. Knopf, 1966). For an African Caribbean religion, see Joseph M. Murphy, *Santería: An African Religion in America* (Boston: Beacon Press, 1988). The concept of mythology as a field of study in and of itself is relatively new to China. Perhaps the best accessible Chinese study of Chinese deities is Yuan Ke, *Dragons and Dynasties: An Introduction to Chinese Mythology*, translated and selected by Kim Echlin and Nie Zhixiong (London: Penguin Books, 1993). Descriptions and brief biographies of Chinese deities will be found in E. T. C. Werner, *A Dictionary of Chinese Mythology* (New York: Julian Press, 1961). For Chinese mediumism, see *Through the Earth Darkly* (see above), as well as the two works mentioned in suggestions for chapter 4. A fascinating example of a deity's autobiography as transcribed by a medium in trance will be found in Terry Kleeman, *A God's Own Tale* (Albany: State University of New York Press, 1994).

Chapter 6

There are psychoanalytical studies of trickster deities, but these do not take the divine element seriously. Most of the relevant myths are told in truncated, expurgated form, removing them from their actuality, particularly if they are analyzed for various purposes. Most anthologies also desacralize the myths by rendering them as "folk tales." Although truncated from the oral versions, the following work still contains much of the spirit of these myths, as they are not expurgated (the traditional scatological elements probably play on the juvenile fascination with bodily functions, leading young children to readily memorize them, as I experienced with my own children): Barry Holston Lopez, *Giving Birth to Thunder, Sleeping with His Daughter: Coyote Builds North America* (New York: Avon Books, 1977). Another work to be recommended, written for use in schools, follows closely the Anishnabe versions as they are currently told to children, save for their shorter length: Dorothy M. Reid, *Tales of Nanabozo* (Toronto: Oxford University Press, 1963). A small number of complete myths regarding Raven can be found in John R. Swanton (collector) & John Enrico (trans. and ed.), *Skidegate Haida Myths and Histories* (Skidegate, BC: Queen Charlotte Islands Museum Press, 1995).

Chapter 7

My purpose is not to pillory any particular individual. However, interested readers will find specific references in my books listed under chapter 1 above, as well as in many of my technical theoretical articles in symposium anthologies and religious studies journals. Among the most influential misinterpretations are the Jesuit *Relations* from China, beginning in the late 16th century, which were extremely influential on European intellectual life thereafter. The Chinese reaction to these interpretations will be found in Jacques Gernet, *China and the Christian Impact*, translated by Janet Lloyd (Cambridge: Cambridge University Press, 1985). Further analyses and references regarding the development of the "Great Spirit" and "Creator" concepts in Native American traditions will be found in Jordan Paper, "the Post-Contact Origin of An American Indian High God: The Suppression on Feminine Spirituality," *American Indian Quarterly* 7/4 (1983): 1–24.

The subtle influences on polytheistic societies of centuries existing within a larger monotheistic cultural framework, as well as the difficulties in the application of categorization, including the typological framework of this book, can be found in three interrelated texts concerning Hopi religion. Two books by Ekkehart Malotki and Michael Lomatuway'ma present the modern Hopi understanding of one of their major deities: *Maasaw: Profile of a Hopi God* and *Stories of Maasaw: A Hopi God* American Tribal Religions vol. 10 [1987] and vol. 11 [1987] respectively; (Lincoln: University of Nebraska Press). A third volume in the series (12 [1987]), more properly belonging to the listings for chapters 3, 5 and 6, is Armin W. Geertz and Michael Lomatuway'ma, *Children of Cottonwood: Piety and Ceremonialism in Hopi Indian Puppetry*. This work presents a Hopi ritual in the context of Hopi understanding of the spirit realm. All three publications are bilingual (English and Hopi).

Chapter 8

Further discussion and references with regard to the relationship between the mystic experience and shamanism and medimism, an aspect of the topic in the chapter's first section will be found in my book *The Mystic Experience: A Descriptive and Comparative Analysis* (see preface for bibliographic details).

Few works originally written in English, of course, contain a fully polytheistic perspective, England having been Christianized long before the English language itself came into being. Translations from other languages often obscure or skew such perspectives, either due to the translator's unconscious biases or ostensibly to make the work intelligible to English language readers. More important, few writers discuss fundamental aspects of their own culture, which are usually taken for granted. The following books are exceptional to the above caveats, but the list is not exhaustive. One of the very few early expressions of a polytheistic sensibility will be found in the already mentioned *The Golden Ass* by Apuleius.

With regard to Chinese culture, Michael Saso went from being an ordained Catholic priest to an initiated Daoist priest. His discussion of the teachings of his Daoist master are fully imbued with that aspect of the Chinese understanding: *The Teachings of the Taoist Master Chuang* (New Haven: Yale University Press, 1978). Chinese mediumism includes spirit writing (writing in possession trance), allowing us to have the autobiographies of deities, a uniquely inside view. For an example, see Terry F. Kleeman, *A God's Own Tale*, mentioned above.

For African Brazilian traditions, refer to the two books mentioned above. Serge Bramly is a journalist who extensively interviewed a Mother of the Gods (the head of a ritual center) and presents her understanding in her own words. Amado's novels are written from an insider's perspective that takes the Candomblé understanding as its basis.

There are numerous books available from South Asian perspectives, but many, particularly those written in English, as discussed in chapter 7, tend to add an Anglo-derived quasi-monotheistic overlay on the premodern Hindu polytheistic perspective. Agahananda Bharati is an Austrian who, as a youth after World War II, having become fluent in the relevant languages, went to India and studied Tantrism. He eventually became recognized in India as a Hindu guru, an extraordinary recognition, and then studied anthropology in the United States, becoming one the mainstays of the social scientific study of religion. His autobiography incorporates the Hindu polytheistic perspective, although his personal focus is on the mystic experience of nothingness. See his *The Ochre Robe: An Autobiography* (London: George Allen and Unwin, 1962).

With regard to Native American understandings, the work mentioned above, *Wizard of the Upper Amazon*, contains the reflections of an old man on his capture as a youth while a rubber worker by Amazonian villagers, his training to be their shaman leader, and his eventual escape back to his life in Hispanic Peru; but the understanding of the Amazonian spirit realm never left him. A rare depiction of a prereservation Native North American understanding will be found in George Horse Capture, ed., *The Seven Visions of Bull Lodge: As Told by His Daughter, Garter Snake* (Lincoln: University of Nebraska Press, 1992 [1980]). Toward the end of his life, Bull Lodge of the White Clay people told his visionary experiences to his daughter, Garter Snake. Near the end of her life (after she had converted to Catholicism), she passed his telling, as well telling of her own ritual roles, to Fred P. Gone, who wrote them down. Eventually the manuscript was edited and published. The work provides the religious understanding of a Plains Native prior to the imposition of Western culture (the added Catholic overlay is minor and readily distinguished). A modern Plains spiritual understanding will be found in a work expressing the thoughts of a Lakota ritual leader: John (Fire) Lame Deer and Richard Erdoes, *Lame Deer: Seeker of Visions* (New York: Simon & Schuster, 1972). A contemporary perspective from an Anishnabe (Ojibwa, Chippewa), maintaining the traditional understandings of the western Great Lakes region, will be found in Ron Geyshick, *Te Bwe Win (Truth)* (Toronto: Summerhill Press, 1989).

Finally, although the work focuses on female deities, religious roles, and understandings, *Through the Earth Darkly*, mentioned above, discusses the polytheistic religious understandings of selected African, African American, Native American, and East Asian cultures. Included in the work are many direct quotations from the women of these cultures.

INDEX

❖